The
Best Of
Vanessa-Ann's
Cross-Stitch
Collection

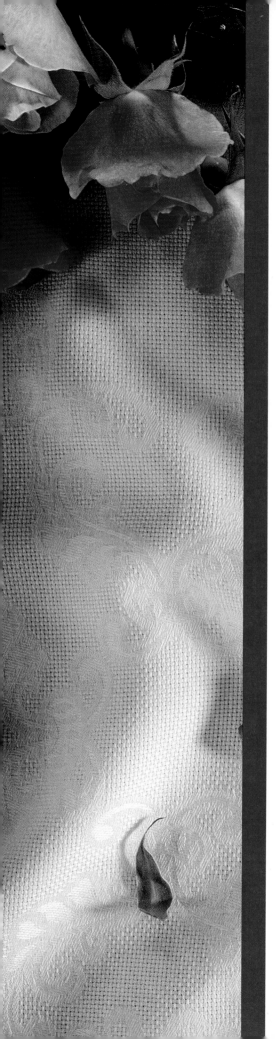
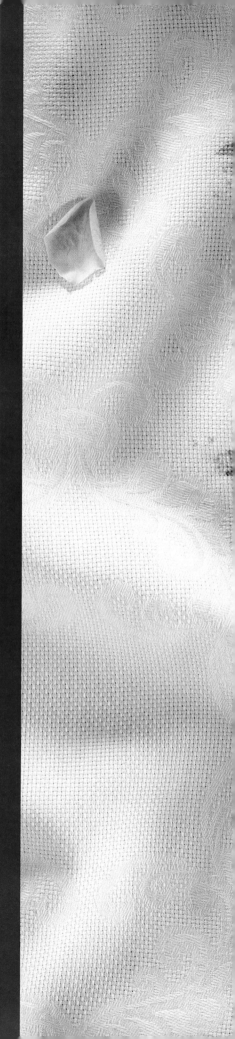

The
Vanessa-Ann Collection

Owners

Jo Packham and Terrece Beesley

Staff

Gloria Zirkel Baur

Sandra D. Chapman

Susan Jorgensen

Margaret Shields Marti

Barbara Milburn

Lisa Miles

Pamela Randall

Lynda Sessions Sorenson

Florence Stacey

Nancy Whitley

Designers

Terrece Beesley

Trice Boerens

Linda Durbano

Tina Richards

Book Design

Baker Design Group

Photographer

Ryne Hazen

The
Best Of
VANESSA-ANN'S
Cross-Stitch
Collection

Dedicated to the memory of my father, Charles Beesley (1913-1975).

©1992 by Oxmoor House, Inc.
Book Division of Southern Progress Corporation
P.O. Box 2463, Birmingham, AL 35201

Library of Congress Catalog Number: 92-80928
ISBN: 0-8487-1112-2
Manufactured in the United States of America

First Printing

Editor-in-Chief: Nancy J. Fitzpatrick
Senior Editor, Editorial Services: Olivia Wells
Director of Manufacturing: Jerry Higdon
Art Director: James Boone

The Best of Vanessa-Ann's Cross-Stitch Collection
from the *Joys of Cross-Stitch* Series

Editor: Laurie Pate Sewell
Editorial Assistant: Shannon Leigh Sexton
Copy Chief: Mary Jean Haddin
Assistant Copy Editor: Susan Smith Cheatham
Production Manager: Rick Litton
Associate Production Manager: Theresa L. Beste
Production Assistant: Pam Beasley Bullock
Designer and Computer Artist: Larry Hunter

The Vanessa-Ann Collection extends its thanks to Trice Boerens, Diana Dunkley,
Penelope Hammons, Nick Kotok, Susan Pendleton, Nan Smith; Kaylene Interiors, Inc.;
Mary Gaskill's Trends and Traditions; The Treasure Basket, Ogden, Utah; The
Bearlace Cottage, Park City, Utah; Brigham Street Inn, Salt Lake City, Utah; and R.C.
Willey Home Furnishings, Syracuse, Utah.
Their trust and cooperation is gratefully acknowledged.

Contents

The Early Years

During the early years, Vanessa-Ann designs were available only in small pamphlets, and until now many of those designs were no longer in print. Here we proudly present some of the best works recaptured just for you in one exciting chapter. A bridal cornucopia filled with an elegant dried floral arrangement will be the perfect wedding keepsake. Trick-or-treat in style with our Halloween brew tote bag. Show a special friend how much you care with a sweet saying surrounded by a vividly stitched rainbow. And, for that precious little baby girl or boy, stitch a birth sampler to record important information.

Homeward Hearts

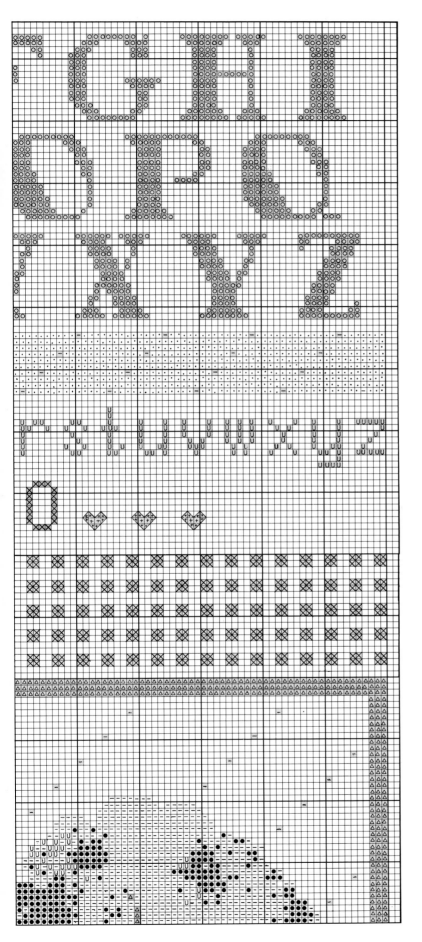

SAMPLE
Stitched on white Belfast Linen 32 over 2 threads, the finished design size is 10⅝" x 17⅛". The fabric was cut 17" x 24".

FABRICS	DESIGN SIZES
Aida 11	15½" x 25⅛"
Aida 14	12⅛" x 19¾"
Aida 18	9½" x 15⅜"
Hardanger 22	7¾" x 12½"

Anchor		DMC (used for sample)	
		Step 1: Cross-stitch (2 strands)	
1		White	
386		746	Off White
300		745	Yellow-lt. pale
297		743	Yellow-med.
303		742	Tangerine-lt.
9		760	Salmon
11		3328	Salmon-dk.
13		347	Salmon-vy. dk.
47		321	Christmas Red
43		815	Garnet-med.
44		814	Garnet-dk.
159		3325	Baby Blue-lt.
145		334	Baby Blue-med.
978		322	Navy Blue-vy. lt.
147		312	Navy Blue-lt.
213		369	Pistachio Green-vy. lt.
214		368	Pistachio Green-lt.
215		320	Pistachio Green-med.
246		319	Pistachio Green-vy. dk.
265		3348	Yellow Green-lt.
257		3346	Hunter Green
227		701	Christmas Green-lt.
370		434	Brown-lt.
349		301	Mahogany-med.
351		400	Mahogany-dk.
378		841	Beige Brown-lt.
379		840	Beige Brown-med.
357		801	Coffee Brown-dk.
905		3031	Mocha Brown-vy. dk.
397		762	Pearl Gray-vy. lt.
400		414	Steel Gray-dk.
401		317	Pewter Gray
		Step 2: Backstitch (1 strand)	
382		3371	Black Brown

Stitch Count: 170 x 276

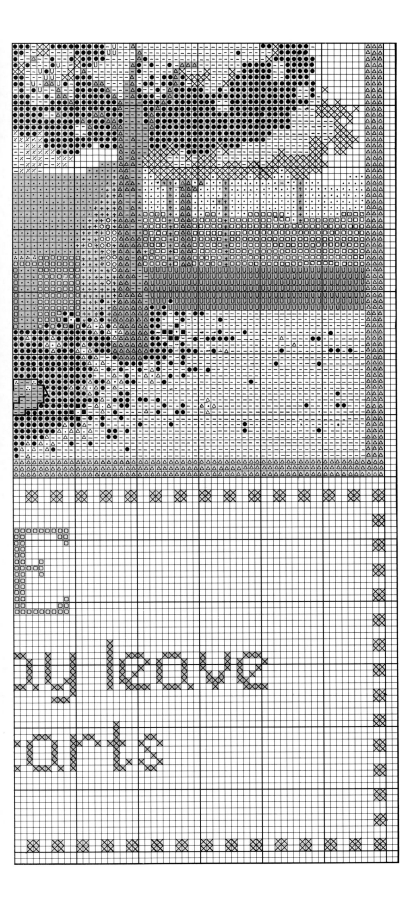

I journeyed to
the rainbow's end
and found not gold
but you my friend

Rainbow's End

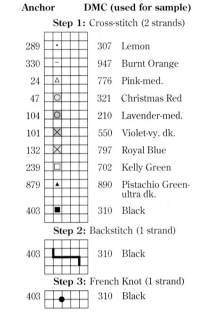

Anchor		DMC (used for sample)	
		Step 1: Cross-stitch (2 strands)	
289	·	307	Lemon
330	–	947	Burnt Orange
24	△	776	Pink-med.
47	○	321	Christmas Red
104	◎	210	Lavender-med.
101	⊠	550	Violet-vy. dk.
132	✕	797	Royal Blue
239	☐	702	Kelly Green
879	▲	890	Pistachio Green-ultra dk.
403	■	310	Black
		Step 2: Backstitch (1 strand)	
403	└	310	Black
		Step 3: French Knot (1 strand)	
403	●	310	Black

Stitch Count: 74 x 81

SAMPLE
Stitched on white Aida 14 over 1 thread, the finished design size is 5¼" x 5¾". The fabric was cut 12" x 12".

FABRICS	DESIGN SIZES
Aida 11	6¾" x 7⅜"
Aida 18	4⅛" x 4½"
Hardanger 22	3⅜" x 3⅝"

Birth Announcements

SAMPLE

Stitched on white Aida 18 over 1 thread, the finished design size for each is 8" x 10⅜". The fabric was cut 14" x 17". To personalize the sampler, transfer the letters and the numerals to graph paper. Mark the center of the graph and begin stitching in the center of the space indicated for personalizing.

FABRICS	DESIGN SIZES
Aida 11	13⅛" x 16⅞"
Aida 14	10¼" x 13¼"
Hardanger 22	6½" x 8½"

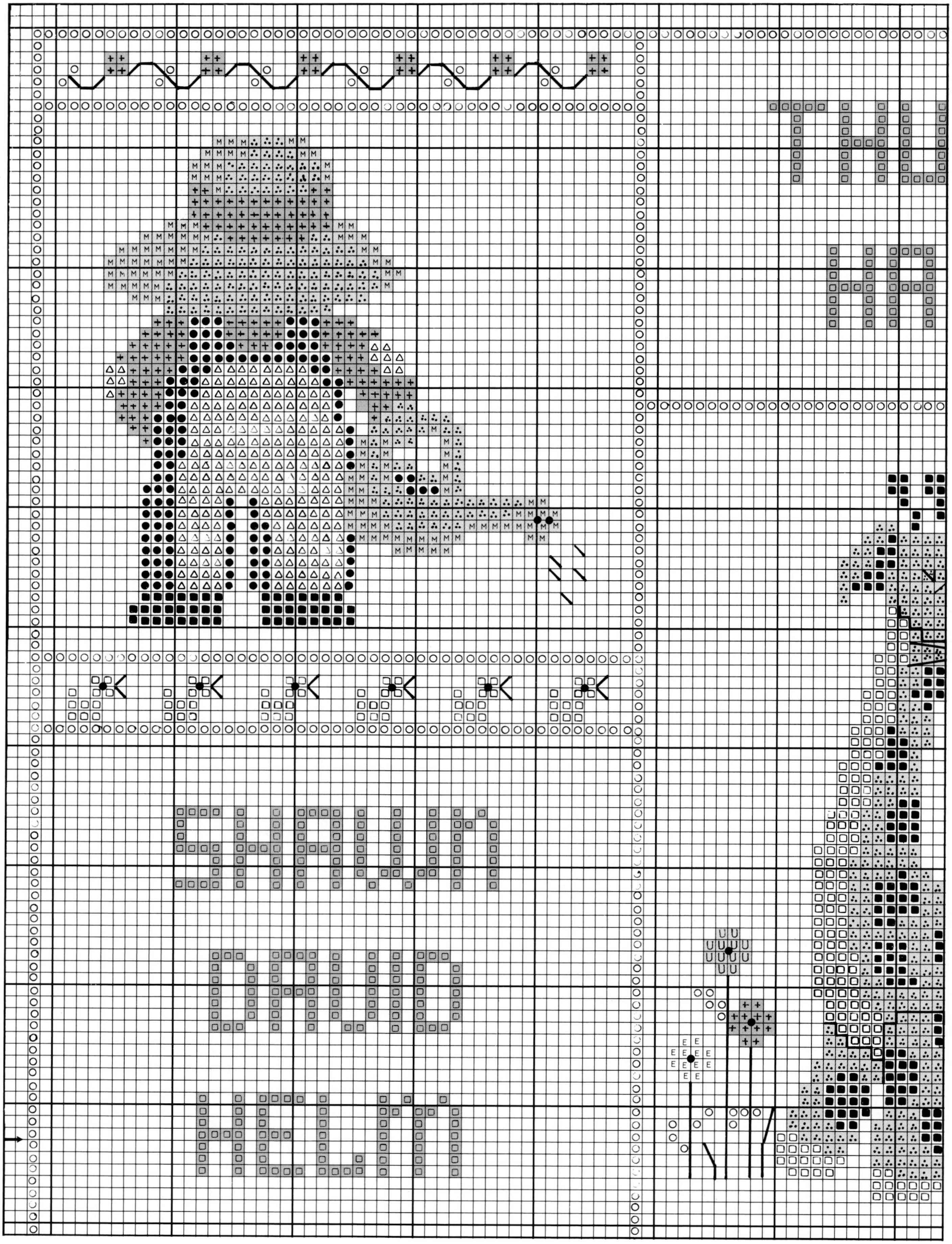

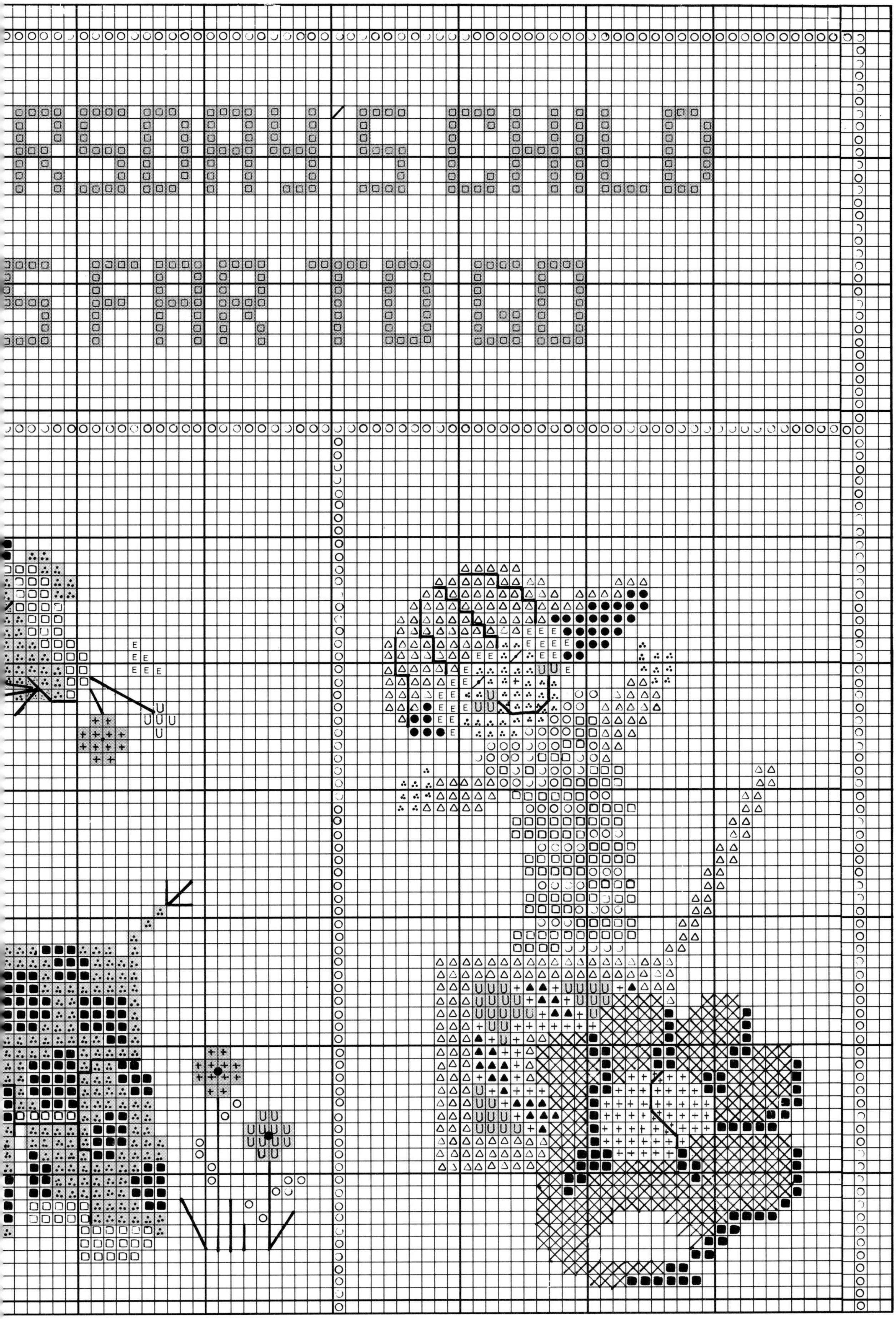

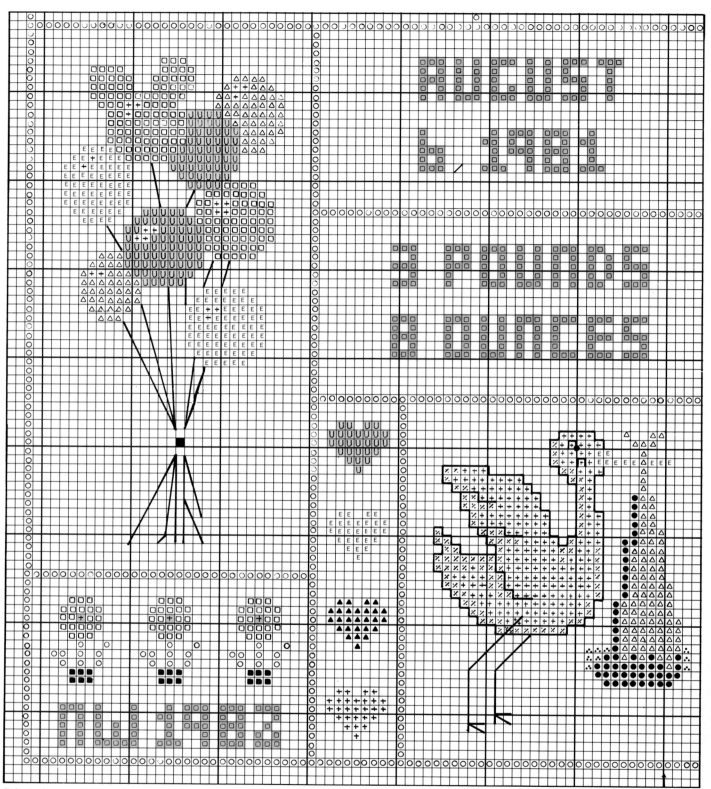

Stitch Count: 144 x 186 (Boy Announcement)

Anchor		DMC (used for sample)
Step 1: Cross-stitch (2 strands)		
1	+	White
297	□	743 Yellow-med.
4146	∴	754 Peach-lt.
333	E	608 Orange Red
335	+	606 Orange Red-bright
76	U /	603 Cranberry
98	▲	553 Violet-med.

160	△	813 Blue-lt.
162	●	825 Blue-dk.
239	O	702 Kelly Green
307	∴	977 Golden Brown-lt.
308	M	976 Golden Brown-med.
308	▣	976 Golden Brown-med.
349	✕	301 Mahogany-med.
352	■	300 Mahogany-vy. dk.

382	⁄	3371 Black Brown
398	╱	415 Pearl Gray
Step 2: Backstitch (1 strand)		
333	▬	608 Orange Red (duck bills, stork legs, white edges of "C")
76	▬	603 Cranberry (mouth on jack-in-the-box)
160	▬	813 Blue-lt. (white edges of rattle)

18

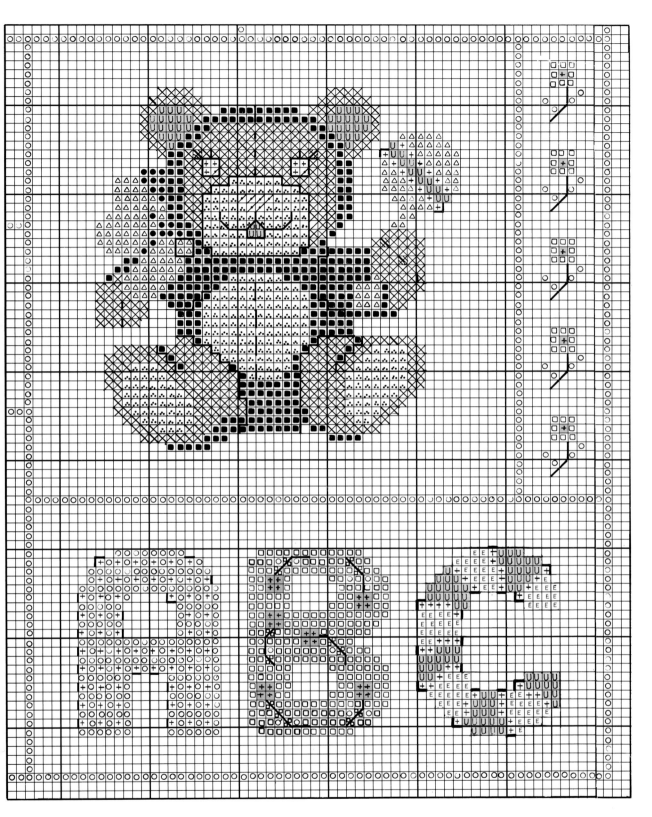

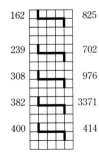

162		825	Blue-dk. (water drops, center of bear bow, jack-in-the box hat)
239		702	Kelly Green (stems, white edges of "A")
308		976	Golden Brown-med. (brown lettering)
382		3371	Black Brown (giraffe, glove center, bear)
400		414	Steel Gray-dk. (stork body, mouth, eye)

Step 3: French Knot (1 strand)

297	●	743	Yellow-med. (flower centers)
162	●	825	Blue-dk. (duck eyes)
352	●	300	Mahogany-vy. dk. (watering can holes)
400	●	414	Steel Gray-dk. (stork eyes)

Step 4: Long Stitch (1 strand)

239	╱	702	Kelly Green (flower stems in giraffe box)
307	╱	977	Golden Brown-lt. (giraffe tail)
382	╱	3371	Black Brown (balloon strings)

Step 5: Bow Placement

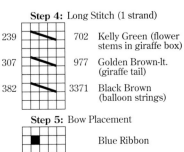

Blue Ribbon

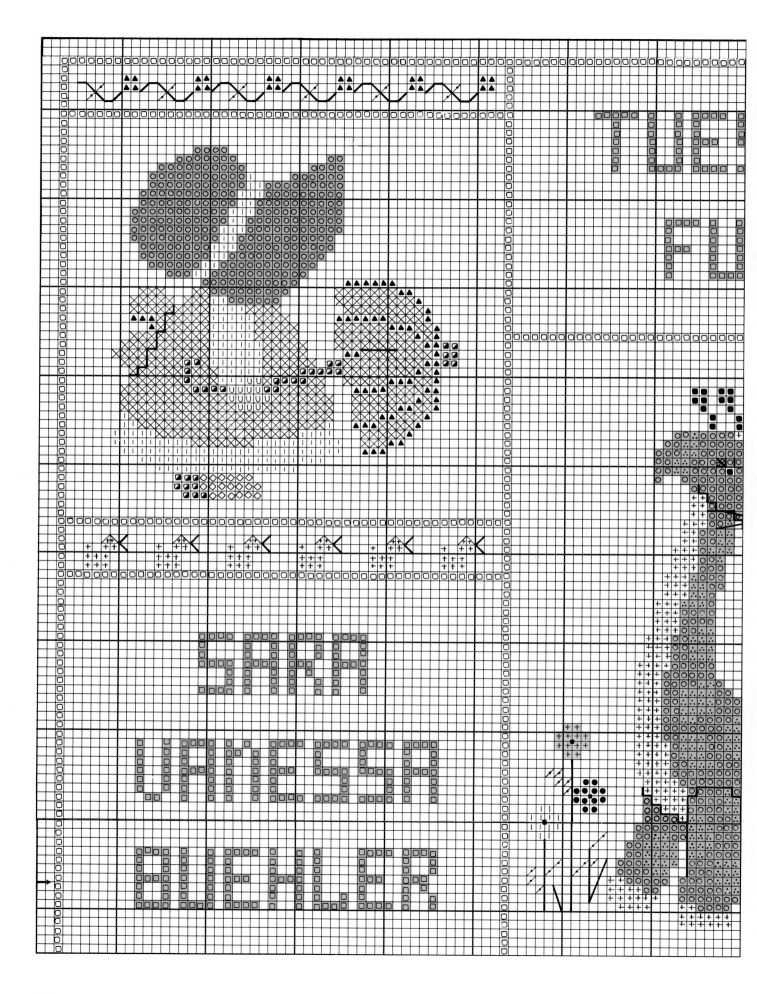

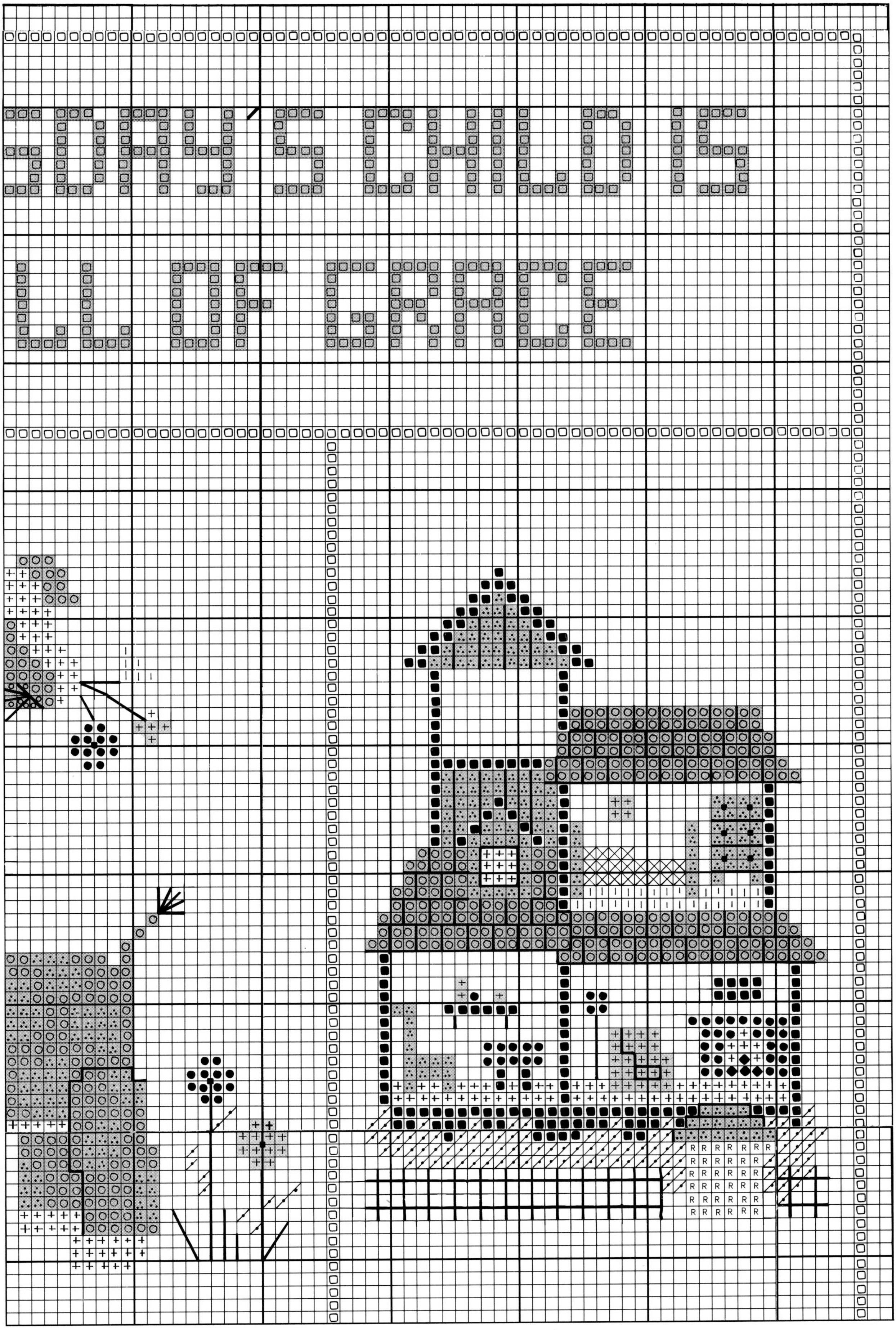
DAY'S CHILD IS
OF GRACE

Stitch Count 144 x 186 (Girl Announcement)

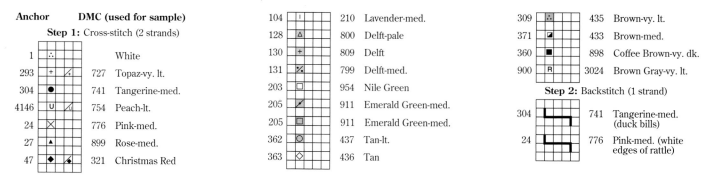

Anchor		DMC (used for sample)								
		Step 1: Cross-stitch (2 strands)	104		210	Lavender-med.	309		435	Brown-vy. lt.
			128		800	Delft-pale	371		433	Brown-med.
1		White	130		809	Delft	360		898	Coffee Brown-vy. dk.
293		727 Topaz-vy. lt.	131		799	Delft-med.	900	R	3024	Brown Gray-vy. lt.
304	●	741 Tangerine-med.	203		954	Nile Green				
4146	U	754 Peach-lt.	205		911	Emerald Green-med.			**Step 2:** Backstitch (1 strand)	
24	✕	776 Pink-med.	205		911	Emerald Green-med.	304		741	Tangerine-med. (duck bills)
27	▲	899 Rose-med.	362	○	437	Tan-lt.	24		776	Pink-med. (white edges of rattle)
47	◆	321 Christmas Red	363	◇	436	Tan				

22

		899	Rose-med. (dress, heart in rainbow)			433	Brown-med. (giraffe)
27				371			
104		210	Lavender-med. (white edges of "A")	357		801	Coffee Brown-dk. (bear)
128		800	Delft-pale (white edges of "C")	360		898	Coffee Brown-vy. dk. (house)
131		799	Delft-med. (center of bear bow)	900		3024	Brown Gray-vy. lt. (fence)
205		911	Emerald Green-med. (stems, lettering)				
362		437	Tan-lt. (giraffe's tail)				

Step 3: French Knot (1 strand)

360		898	Coffee Brown-vy. dk.

Step 4: Long Stitch (1 strand)

205		911	Emerald Green-med. (flower stems in giraffe box)
403		310	Black (balloon strings)

Step 5: Bow Placement

Pink Ribbon

23

Monday's Child is fair of face.

Tuesday's child is full of grace.

Wednesday's child is full of woe.

Thursday's child has far to go.

Friday's child works hard for a living.

Saturday's child is loving and giving.

And the child that's born on the Sabbath day

Is bonny and blythe in every way.

Something's Brewing

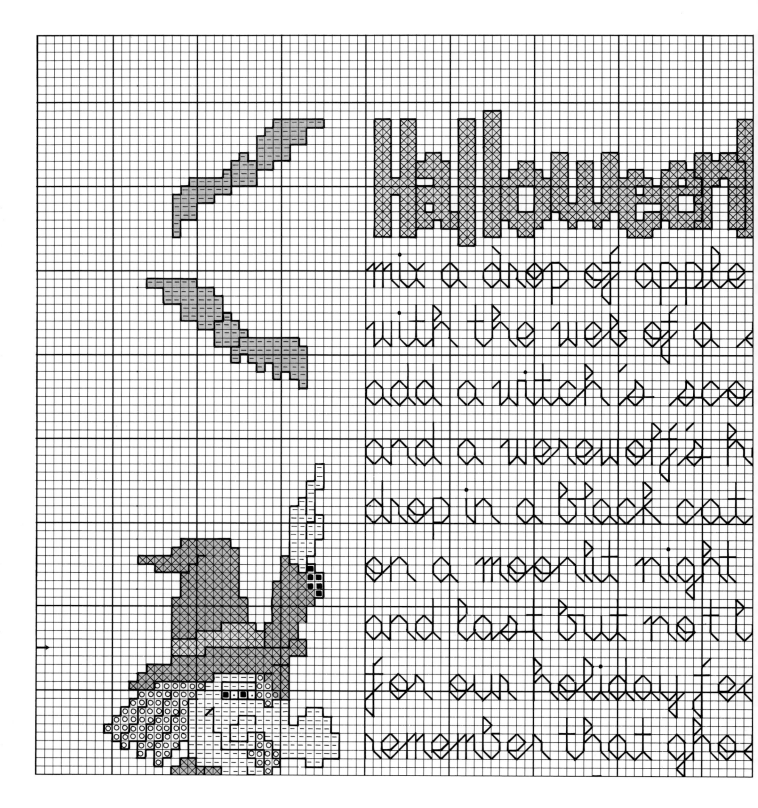

SAMPLE
Stitched on white Aida 14 over 1 thread, the finished design size is 9⅞" x 10⅛". The fabric was cut 16" x 17".

FABRICS	DESIGN SIZES
Aida 11	12½" x 12⅞"
Aida 18	7⅝" x 7⅞"
Hardanger 22	6¼" x 6½"

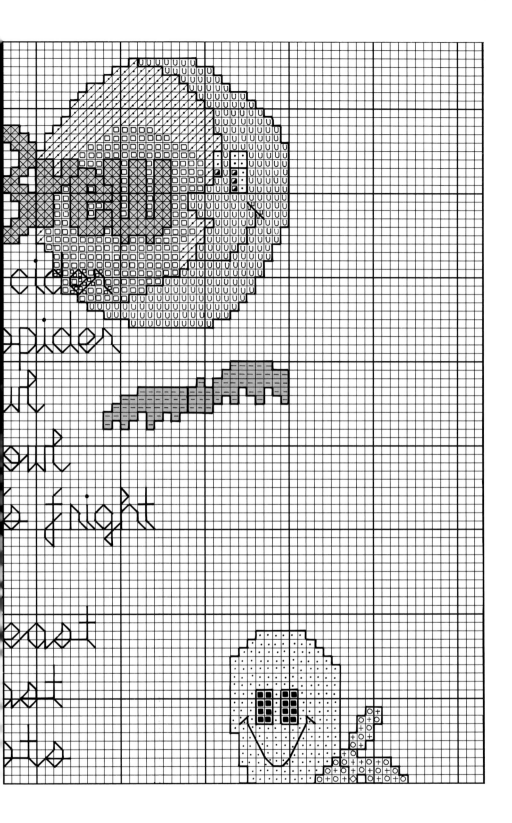

Stitch Count: 138 x 142

MATERIALS
Completed cross-stitch design on white Aida 14; matching thread
½ yard of unstitched white Aida 14
½ yard of Halloween print fabric; matching thread
½ yard of polyester fleece

DIRECTIONS
All seam allowances are ¼".

1. For bag front, with design centered, trim Aida to a 14½" square. From unstitched Aida, cut 1 (14½") square for back and 2 (3½" x 19") pieces for handles. From print fabric, cut 2 (14½") squares for lining. From fleece, cut 2 (14½") squares.

2. Baste 1 fleece square each to wrong side of bag front and back. With right sides facing and raw edges aligned, stitch bag front and back together around side and bottom edges, leaving top edge open. Trim batting from seam.

3. To make a boxed bottom, at 1 bottom corner of bag, align side and bottom seams by flattening bag, with right sides facing and with 1 seam on top of the other; finger-press seam allowances open. Stitch across corner as shown in Diagram. Repeat for other bottom corner. Clip corners and turn.

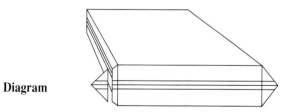

Diagram

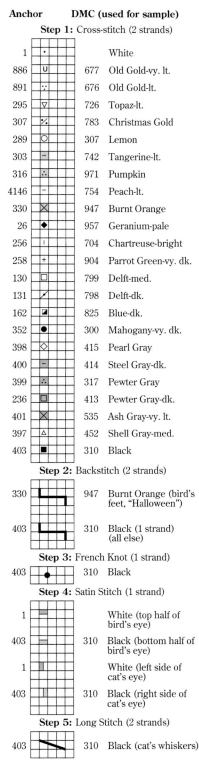

Anchor		DMC	(used for sample)
		Step 1: Cross-stitch (2 strands)	
1	·		White
886	U	677	Old Gold-vy. lt.
891	∴	676	Old Gold-lt.
295	▽	726	Topaz-lt.
307	⅍	783	Christmas Gold
289	○	307	Lemon
303	–	742	Tangerine-lt.
316	∴	971	Pumpkin
4146	–	754	Peach-lt.
330	✕	947	Burnt Orange
26	◆	957	Geranium-pale
256	I	704	Chartreuse-bright
258	+	904	Parrot Green-vy. dk.
130	□	799	Delft-med.
131	╱	798	Delft-dk.
162	◪	825	Blue-dk.
352	●	300	Mahogany-vy. dk.
398	◇	415	Pearl Gray
400	▬	414	Steel Gray-dk.
399	∴	317	Pewter Gray
236	▢	413	Pewter Gray-dk.
401	✕	535	Ash Gray-vy. lt.
397	△	452	Shell Gray-med.
403	■	310	Black

Step 2: Backstitch (2 strands)

330		947	Burnt Orange (bird's feet, "Halloween")
403		310	Black (1 strand) (all else)

Step 3: French Knot (1 strand)

403	●	310	Black

Step 4: Satin Stitch (1 strand)

1			White (top half of bird's eye)
403		310	Black (bottom half of bird's eye)
1			White (left side of cat's eye)
403		310	Black (right side of cat's eye)

Step 5: Long Stitch (2 strands)

403	╲	310	Black (cat's whiskers)

4. For lining, with right sides facing and raw edges aligned, stitch printed pieces together around side and bottom edges, leaving an opening in side seam. Referring to step 3 above, make boxed bottom. Do not turn lining.

5. To make handles, fold 1 (3½" x 19") piece in half lengthwise. Stitch long edges together. Turn. Press with seam centered. With right sides facing and raw edges aligned, pin each end of handle 3" from each side seam to top edge of bag front. Baste ends in place. Repeat with remaining handle on bag back. With right sides facing and seams aligned, slip lining over bag. Stitch around top edge, catching handles in seam. Turn through opening in lining. Tuck lining inside bag.

A Gift from the Heart

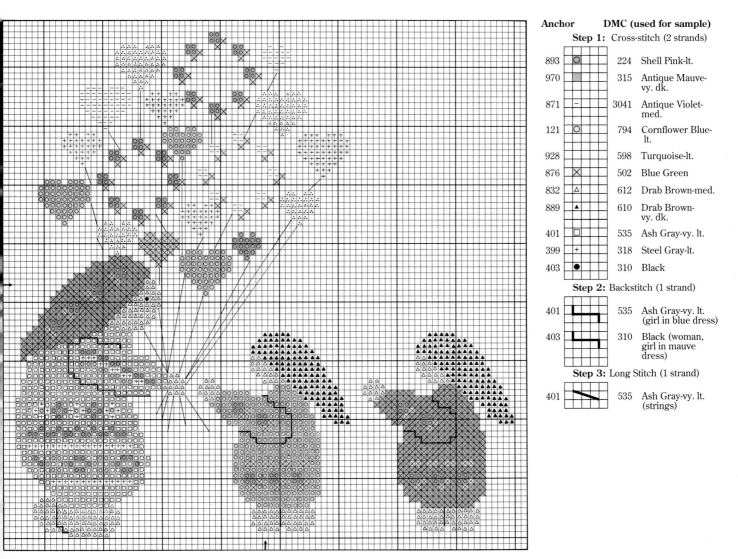

Anchor		DMC (used for sample)	
Step 1: Cross-stitch (2 strands)			
893	○	224	Shell Pink-lt.
970	▨	315	Antique Mauve-vy. dk.
871	–	3041	Antique Violet-med.
121	⊙	794	Cornflower Blue-lt.
928	⊙	598	Turquoise-lt.
876	✕	502	Blue Green
832	△	612	Drab Brown-med.
889	▲	610	Drab Brown-vy. dk.
401	□	535	Ash Gray-vy. lt.
399	+	318	Steel Gray-lt.
403	●	310	Black
Step 2: Backstitch (1 strand)			
401		535	Ash Gray-vy. lt. (girl in blue dress)
403		310	Black (woman, girl in mauve dress)
Step 3: Long Stitch (1 strand)			
401		535	Ash Gray-vy. lt. (strings)

Stitch Count: 85 x 86

SAMPLE
Stitched on white Linda 27 over 2 threads, the finished design size is 6¼" x 6⅜". The fabric was cut 12" x 12".

FABRICS	DESIGN SIZES
Aida 11	7¾" x 7⅞"
Aida 14	6⅛" x 6⅛"
Aida 18	4¾" x 4¾"
Hardanger 22	3⅞" x 3⅞"

Folk Sampler

SAMPLE

Stitched on beige Hardanger 22 over 1 and 2 threads, the finished design size is 15⅜" x 26⅜". The fabric was cut 22" x 33". Use 1 strand of embroidery floss when stitching over 1 thread and 2 strands when stitching over 2 threads. Note that sections stitched over 1 thread have a smaller grid than those stitched over 2 threads. To accommodate the 2 sizes of stitches, this design must be stitched on monoweave fabric. To personalize the sampler, transfer letters and numerals to graph paper. Mark center of graph and begin stitching in center of space indicated for personalizing.

FABRICS	DESIGN SIZES
Linda 27	12½" x 21½"
Murano 30	11¼" x 19⅜"
Belfast Linen 32	10½" x 18⅛"

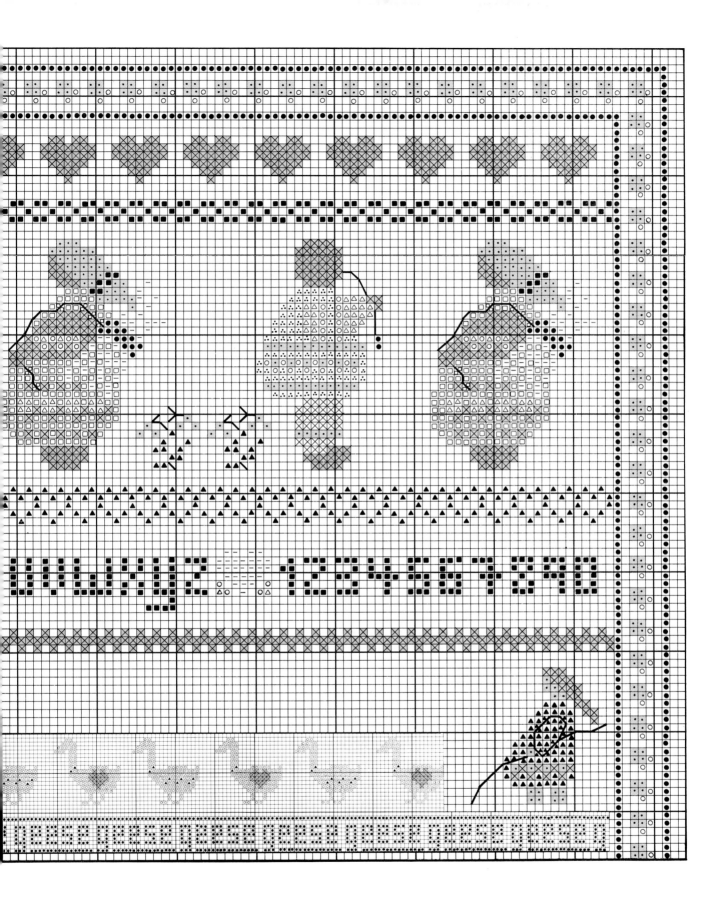

35

37

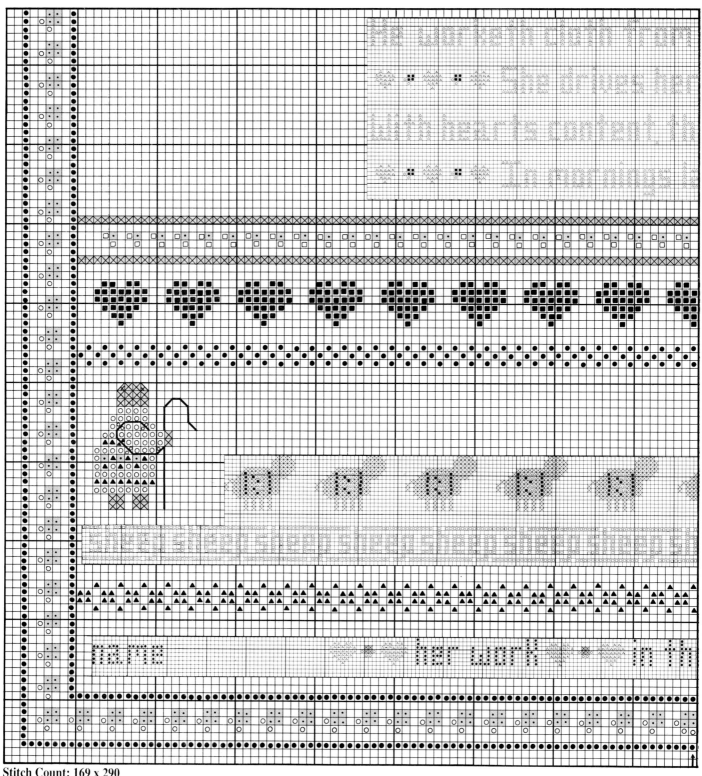

Stitch Count: 169 x 290

Anchor		DMC (used for sample)
Step 1: Cross-stitch (2 strands)		
969	△	316 Antique Mauve-med.
970	⠘	315 Antique Mauve-vy. dk.
871	·	3041 Antique Violet-med.
150	●	823 Navy Blue-dk.
849	⨯	927 Slate Green-med.

779	■	926 Slate Green
851	☐	924 Slate Green-vy. dk.
859	○ /	3052 Green Gray-med.
862	▲	934 Black Avocado Green
832	·	612 Drab Brown-med.
889	⨯	610 Drab Brown-vy. dk.

944	−	869 Hazel Nut Brown-vy. dk.
401	⨯	413 Pewter Gray-dk.

Step 2: Backstitch (1 strand)

150	⌐	823 Navy Blue-dk. (people, pipes, rope, cane, window)

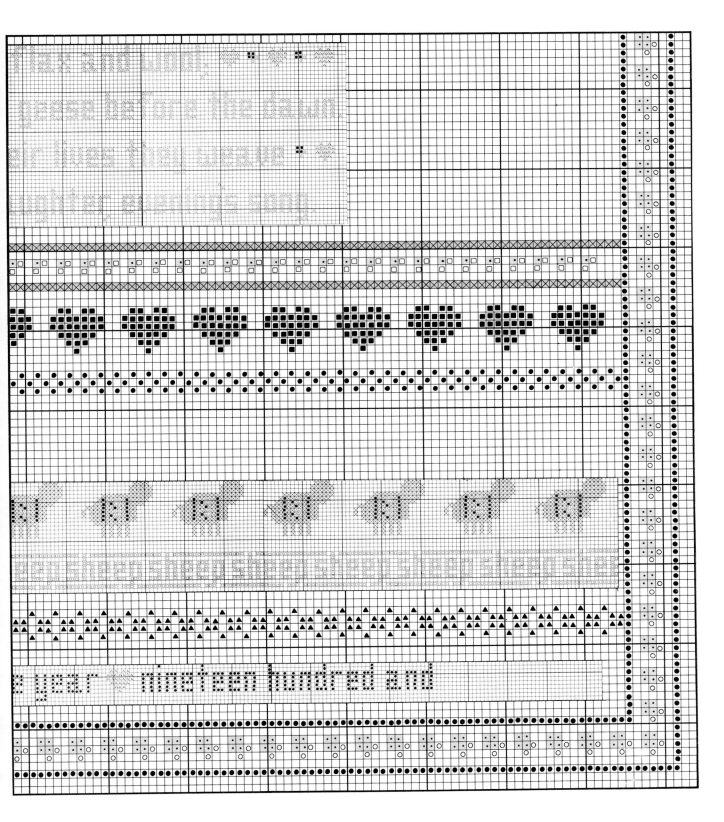

862 | 934 Black Avocado Green
(flower stems)

72 | 902 Garnet-vy. dk.
(ties on stalks)

Step 3: Long Stitch (1 strand)

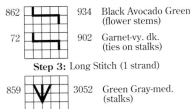

859 | 3052 Green Gray-med.
(stalks)

Wedding Keepsake

SAMPLE

Stitched on white Belfast Linen 32 over 2 threads, the finished design size is 8" x 4⅜". The fabric was cut 15" x 15".

FABRICS	DESIGN SIZES
Aida 11	11½" x 6⅜"
Aida 14	9⅛" x 5"
Aida 18	7" x 3⅞"
Hardanger 22	5¼" x 3⅛"

Stitch Count: 127 x 70

MATERIALS

Completed design on white Belfast Linen 32; matching thread
15" square of white fabric for lining
2 (15") squares of heavy crinoline
¾ yard (¾"-wide) double-edged gold trim
Dried flower bouquet

DIRECTIONS

All seam allowances are ¼".

1. Enlarge pattern. Place pattern on design piece with top edge of pattern 1½" above and parallel to top row of stitching. Cut out. From white fabric, cut 1 piece for lining. From crinoline, cut 2 pieces ¼" smaller all around than pattern.

2. With right sides facing, stitch design piece and lining together, leaving 1 straight edge open. Clip corners and turn. Handling crinoline pieces as 1, insert between design piece and lining, fitting carefully into corners. Turn under seam allowance and slipstitch opening closed.

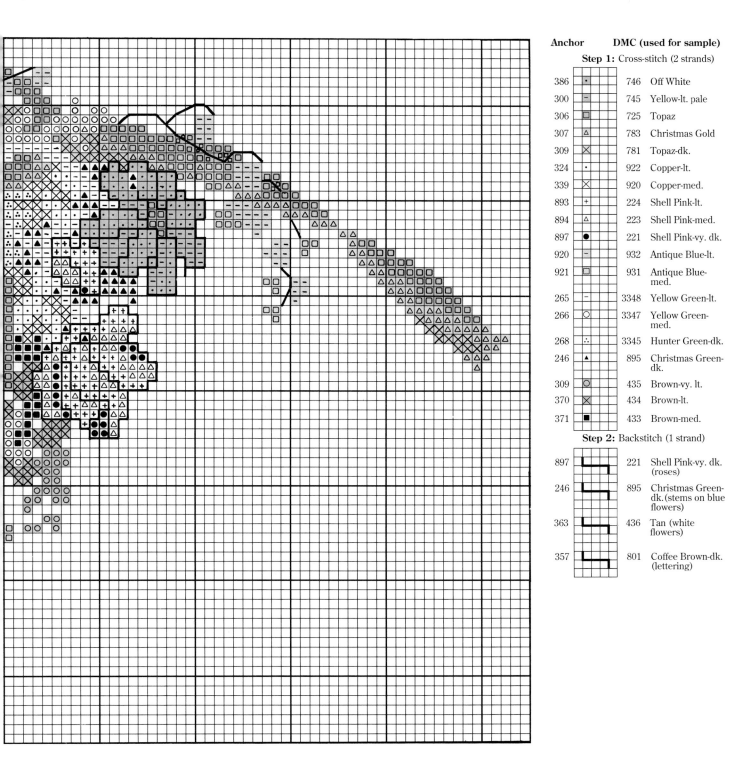

Anchor		DMC	(used for sample)
		Step 1: Cross-stitch (2 strands)	
386	•	746	Off White
300	−	745	Yellow-lt. pale
306	▫	725	Topaz
307	△	783	Christmas Gold
309	✕	781	Topaz-dk.
324	·	922	Copper-lt.
339	✕	920	Copper-med.
893	+	224	Shell Pink-lt.
894	△	223	Shell Pink-med.
897	●	221	Shell Pink-vy. dk.
920	−	932	Antique Blue-lt.
921	▫	931	Antique Blue-med.
265	−	3348	Yellow Green-lt.
266	○	3347	Yellow Green-med.
268	∴	3345	Hunter Green-dk.
246	▲	895	Christmas Green-dk.
309	○	435	Brown-vy. lt.
370	✕	434	Brown-lt.
371	■	433	Brown-med.

		Step 2: Backstitch (1 strand)	
897	⌐	221	Shell Pink-vy. dk. (roses)
246	⌐	895	Christmas Green-dk.(stems on blue flowers)
363	⌐	436	Tan (white flowers)
357	⌐	801	Coffee Brown-dk. (lettering)

3. To form cornucopia, carefully roll design piece into a cone, overlapping straight edges ½". Slipstitch straight edges together.

4. Tack gold trim around top edge and down center back seam. Fill with dried flower bouquet.

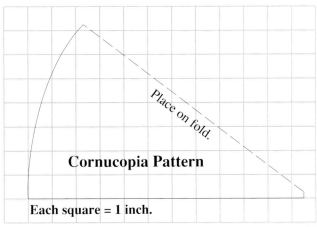

Cornucopia Pattern

Place on fold.

Each square = 1 inch.

From The Heart

Sentiments can be expressed
in many different ways—a
friendly gesture, a kind word,
or a special handmade gift.
In this chapter, you'll find a
collection of designs that will
help convey your feelings.
An elegant sampler showing
the names and birthdates of those
special grandchildren is sure to
be a treasure for Grandma and
Grandpa. A richly colored
table runner will add warmth
to the family's Thanksgiving
dinner. Greet your friends
with a floral wreath that spells
out "Welcome," or stitch up
an extra-special piece that
says "I Love You" for
someone dear.

My Grandchildren

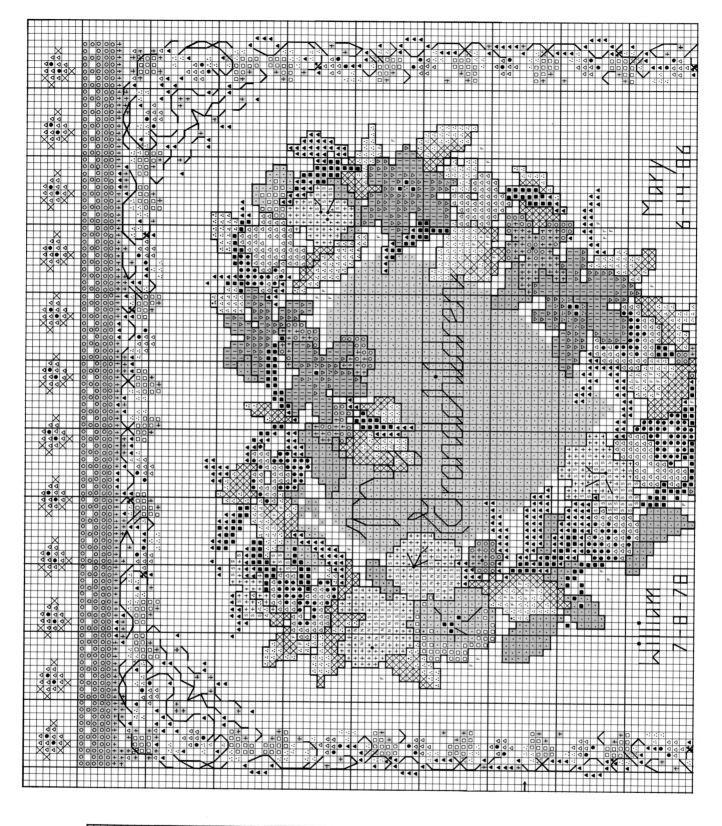

Stitch Count: 109 x 143

Stephen 3-13-85

Alex 2-21-84

Debra 8-10-82

Sally 12-2-80

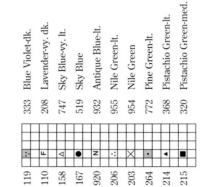

Anchor		DMC (used for sample)	
Step 1:		Cross-stitch (2 strands)	
300	•	745	Yellow-lt. pale
301	□	744	Yellow-pale
8	+	353	Peach
328	s	3341	Apricot
24	+	776	Pink-med.
76	O	962	Wild Rose-med.
117	I	341	Blue Violet-lt.
118		340	Blue Violet-med.
119	::	333	Blue Violet-dk.
110	F	208	Lavender-vy. dk.
158	△	747	Sky Blue-vy. lt.
167	●	519	Sky Blue
920	N	932	Antique Blue-lt.
206	::	955	Nile Green-lt.
203	X	954	Nile Green
264		772	Pine Green-lt.
214	•	368	Pistachio Green-lt.
215	■	320	Pistachio Green-med.

Step 2: Backstitch (1 strand)

168	518	Wedgwood-lt. (outside border)
216	367	Pistachio Green-dk. (large flowers, leaves forming heart)
246	319	Pistachio Green-vy. dk. ("My Grandchildren", names, dates)

Step 3: French Knot (1 strand)

216	367	Pistachio Green-dk.
246	319	Pistachio Green-vy. dk.

SAMPLE

Stitched on cream Belfast Linen 32 over 2 threads, the finished design size is 6¾" x 9". The fabric was cut 13" x 15". To personalize the design, transfer names and dates of birth to graph paper, centering each date below corresponding name. Mark the center of the graph and begin stitching in the center of the space indicated.

FABRICS

DESIGN SIZES

Aida 11	9⅞" x 13"
Aida 14	7¾" x 10¼"
Aida 18	6" x 8"
Hardanger 22	5" x 6½"

I Love You

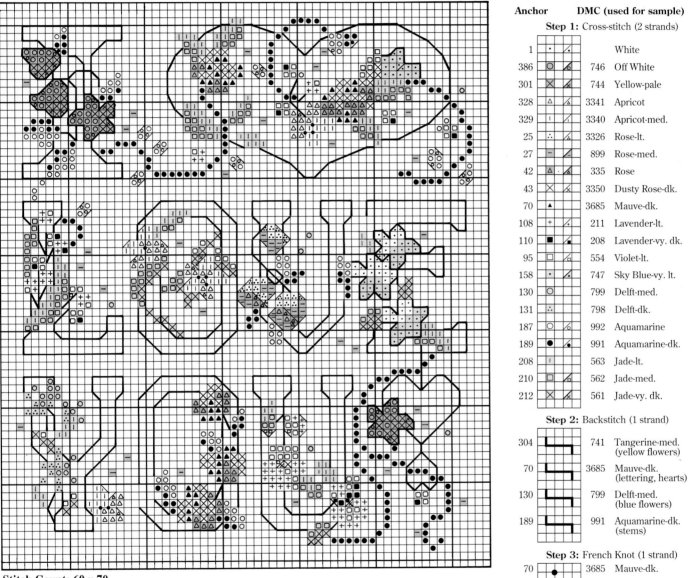

Stitch Count: 60 x 70

Anchor			DMC (used for sample)	
			Step 1: Cross-stitch (2 strands)	
1	·	∕		White
386	○	∕	746	Off White
301	✕	∕	744	Yellow-pale
328	△	∕	3341	Apricot
329	∣	∕	3340	Apricot-med.
25	∴	∕	3326	Rose-lt.
27	▭	∕	899	Rose-med.
42	△	∕	335	Rose
43	✕	∕	3350	Dusty Rose-dk.
70	▲		3685	Mauve-dk.
108	+	∕	211	Lavender-lt.
110	■	∕	208	Lavender-vy. dk.
95	□	∕	554	Violet-lt.
158	·	∕	747	Sky Blue-vy. lt.
130	○		799	Delft-med.
131	∷		798	Delft-dk.
187	○	∕	992	Aquamarine
189	●	∕	991	Aquamarine-dk.
208	∣		563	Jade-lt.
210	□	∕	562	Jade-med.
212	✕	∕	561	Jade-vy. dk.
			Step 2: Backstitch (1 strand)	
304			741	Tangerine-med. (yellow flowers)
70			3685	Mauve-dk. (lettering, hearts)
130			799	Delft-med. (blue flowers)
189			991	Aquamarine-dk. (stems)
			Step 3: French Knot (1 strand)	
70			3685	Mauve-dk.

SAMPLE

Stitched on white Belfast Linen 32 over 2 threads, the finished design size is 3¾" x 4⅜". The fabric was cut 10" x 11".

FABRICS	DESIGN SIZES
Aida 11	5½" x 6⅜"
Aida 14	4¼" x 5"
Aida 18	3⅜" x 3⅞"
Hardanger 22	2¾" x 3⅛"

Special Delivery Cupids

Stitch Count: 94 x 70

SAMPLE

Stitched on white Belfast Linen 32 over 2 threads, the finished design size is 5⅞" x 4⅜". Fabric was cut 12" x 11".

FABRICS	DESIGN SIZES
Aida 11	8½" x 6⅜"
Aida 14	6¾" x 5"
Aida 18	5¼" x 3⅞"
Hardanger 22	4¼" x 3⅛"

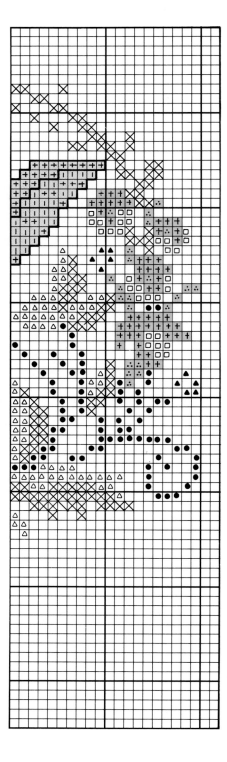

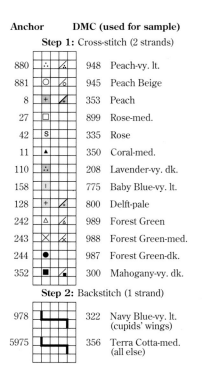

Anchor			DMC (used for sample)	
Step 1: Cross-stitch (2 strands)				
880			948	Peach-vy. lt.
881			945	Peach Beige
8			353	Peach
27			899	Rose-med.
42			335	Rose
11			350	Coral-med.
110			208	Lavender-vy. dk.
158			775	Baby Blue-vy. lt.
128			800	Delft-pale
242			989	Forest Green
243			988	Forest Green-med.
244			987	Forest Green-dk.
352			300	Mahogany-vy. dk.
Step 2: Backstitch (1 strand)				
978			322	Navy Blue-vy. lt. (cupids' wings)
5975			356	Terra Cotta-med. (all else)

Bunny Bouquet

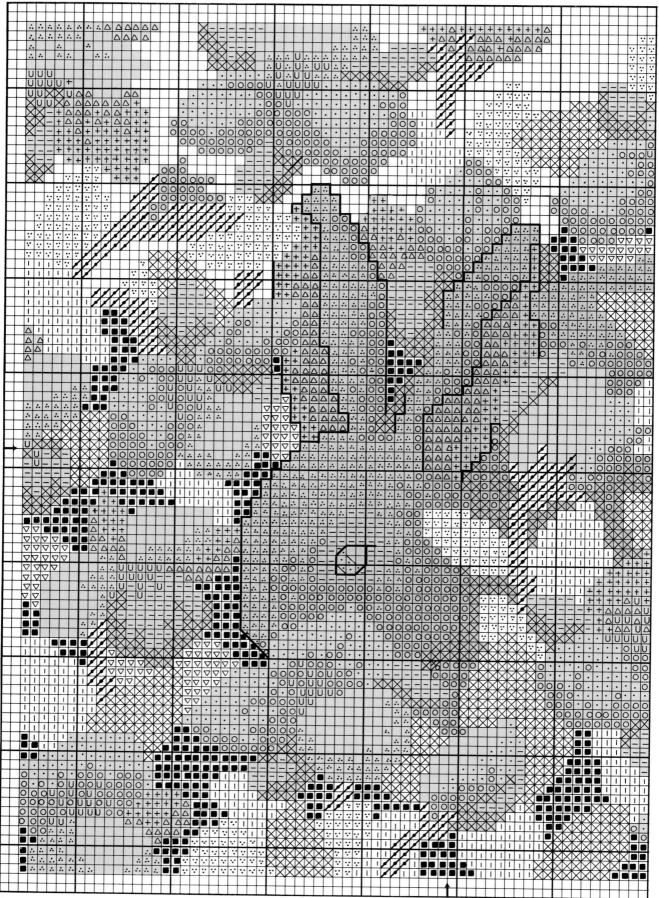

Stitch Count: 90 x 90

SAMPLE

Stitched on Wedgwood Murano 30 over 2 threads, the finished design size is 6" x 6". The fabric was cut 12" x 12".

FABRICS	DESIGN SIZES
Aida 11	8⅛" x 8⅛"
Aida 14	6⅜" x 6⅜"
Aida 18	5" x 5"
Hardanger 22	4⅛" x 4⅛"

Anchor		DMC (used for sample)	
Step 1: Cross-stitch (2 strands)			
303	U	742	Tangerine-lt.
26		3708	Melon-lt.
28	∴	3706	Melon-med.
75	•	604	Cranberry-lt.
76	O	603	Cranberry
86	−	3608	Plum-vy. lt.
87	X	3607	Plum-lt.
95	+	554	Violet-lt.
98	△	553	Violet-med.
186	ı	993	Aquamarine-lt.
203	╱	954	Nile Green
204	X	912	Emerald Green-lt.
210	▽	562	Jade-med.
212	∴	561	Jade-vy. dk.
879	■ ╱	500	Blue Green-vy. dk.
885	+	739	Tan-ultra vy. lt.
942	△	738	Tan-vy. lt.
4146	− ╱	950	Peach Pecan-dk.
914	∴ ╱	3064	Pecan-lt.
914 936	O ╱	3064 632	Pecan-lt. (1 strand) + Pecan-dk. (1 strand)
936	X ╱	632	Pecan-dk.
Step 2: Satin Stitch (1 strand)			
8581	• ╱	3022	Brown Gray-med.
382		3021	Brown Gray-vy. dk.
Step 3: Backstitch (1 strand)			
936		632	Pecan-dk. (bunny ears, head)
382		3021	Brown Gray-vy. dk. (around eye)

Bountiful Harvest Table Runner

SAMPLE

Stitched on Vanessa-Ann Afghan Weave 18 over 1 thread. The fabric was cut 24" x 58" (the width measurement includes 3 whole blocks and ½ block on each side). The stitching area of each woven block is 88 x 88. The heavy black lines surrounding each graph indicate the block boundaries. (See Diagram for placement.) Stitch design on each end of runner. See Suppliers for Afghan material and Overture yarn.

MATERIALS

Completed cross-stitch on Vanessa-Ann Afghan Weave 18; matching thread
Overture variegated yarn: 10 skeins Spices (color V58)
Size 4 steel crochet hook

DIRECTIONS

1. To hem runner, turn under ½" twice along all raw edges, mitering corners. Slipstitch hem in place.

2. *Note:* See page 62 for crochet abbreviations. Separate yarn into 4 single strands. Work first row of crochet stitches under 2 or 3 threads of fabric at folded edge of hem. *Row 1:* With runner turned to work across 1 cross-stitched end, join 1 strand of yarn in corner, sc in same place, * ch 5, sk 13 or 14 threads, sc between next 2 threads, rep from * across, end with sc in corner = 30 sc and 29 ch-5 sps. Turn. *Row 2:* Sl st into ch-5 sp, ch 3 for first dc, 3 dc in same sp, * ch 3, 4 dc in next sp, rep from * across = 29 4-dc groups. Turn. *Row 3: Beginning half-triangle:* Ch 6 for first dc and ch 3, 4 dc in next sp, ch 3, 4 dc in next sp, turn, sl st into next ch-3 sp, ch 3 for dc, 3 dc in same sp, ch 3, 4 dc in next sp, turn, ch 6 for dc and ch 3, 4 dc in next sp. Fasten off. *Triangle:* Sk next 4-dc group on row 2, join yarn in next ch-3 sp, ch 3 for first dc, 3 dc in same sp, (ch 3, 4 dc in next sp) 7 times, turn, * sl st into next ch-3 sp, ch 3 for first dc, 3 dc in same sp, (ch 3, 4 dc in next sp) across, turn, rep from * 5 times more. Fasten off. Rep triangle as established twice more. *Ending half-triangle:* Sk next 4-dc group on Row 2, join yarn in next ch-3 sp, ch 3 for first dc, 3 dc in same sp, ch 3, 4 dc in next sp, ch 3, sk 3 dc, dc in next dc, turn, ch 3 for dc, 3 dc in sp, ch 3, 4 dc in next sp, turn, sl st into next ch-3 sp, ch 3 for dc, 3 dc in same sp, ch 3, sk 3 dc, dc in next dc. Fasten off. Repeat for remaining end of runner.

3. For each tassel, cut 5 (18") lengths of yarn (do not separate plies). Make 10 tassels. Knot a tassel in the ch-3 sp at the point of each triangle and half-triangle on each end of runner.

Anchor		DMC (used for sample)	
		Step 1: Cross-stitch (2 strands)	
300	Z	745	Yellow-lt. pale
293	˅	727	Topaz-vy. lt.
293	⁄	727	Topaz-vy. lt. (1 strand) +
265		3348	Yellow Green-lt. (1 strand)
293	=	727	Topaz-vy. lt. (1 strand) +
8		353	Peach (1 strand)
295	G	726	Topaz-lt.
306	R	725	Topaz
891	W	676	Old Gold-lt.
881	+	945	Peach Beige
8	J	353	Peach
10	◇	352	Coral-lt.
11	N	350	Coral-med.
13	F	349	Coral-dk.
9	∴	3712	Salmon-med.
316	•	971	Pumpkin
323	U	922	Copper-lt.
324	I	721	Orange Spice-med.
326	O	720	Orange Spice-dk.
347	S	402	Mahogany-vy. lt.
339	✕	920	Copper-med.
46	⊡	666	Christmas Red-bright
47	M	321	Christmas Red
42	△	335	Rose
59	✕	326	Rose-vy. dk.
20	◆	498	Christmas Red-dk.
44	●	815	Garnet-med.
43	+	3350	Dusty Rose-dk.
69	∗	3687	Mauve
70	✕	3685	Mauve-dk.
970	▢	315	Antique Mauve-vy. dk.
101	△	327	Antique Violet-vy. dk.
89	U	915	Plum-dk. (1 strand) +
101		327	Antique Violet-vy. dk. (1 strand)

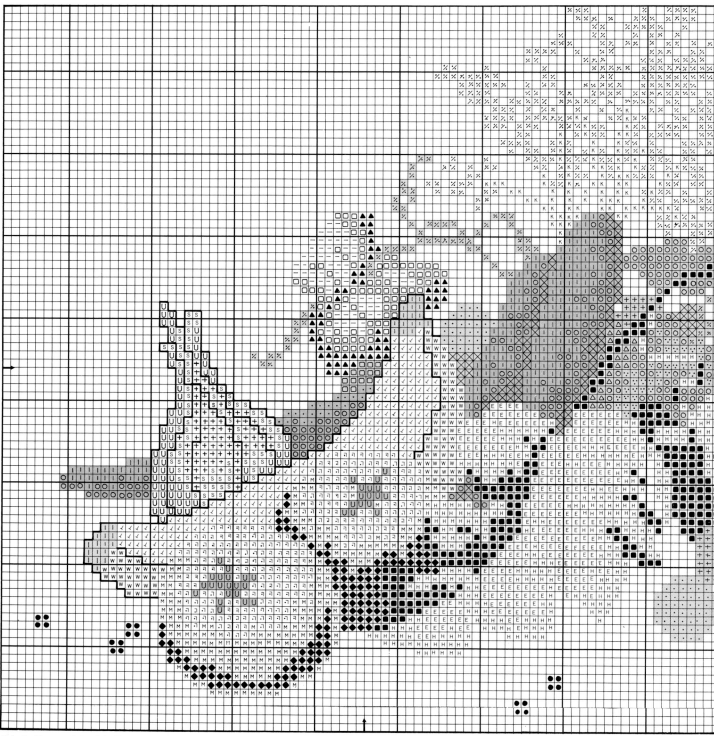

Stitch Count: 84 x 86 (Section A)

264		772	Pine Green-lt.	
265	○	3348	Yellow Green-lt.	
266	E	3347	Yellow Green-med.	
257	H	3346	Hunter Green	
266	K	471	Avocado Green-vy. lt.	
267	⁒	469	Avocado Green	
876	○	502	Blue Green	
878	∴	501	Blue Green-dk.	
210	U	562	Jade-med.	
212	▢	561	Jade-vy. dk.	

215	+	320	Pistachio Green-med.	
216	△	367	Pistachio Green-dk.	
246	∴	319	Pistachio Green-vy. dk.	
843	−	3364	Pine Green	
861	□	3363	Pine Green-med.	
846	■	3051	Green Gray-dk.	
862	▲	520	Fern Green-dk.	
307	B	977	Golden Brown-lt.	
363	I	436	Tan	
375	⁒	420	Hazel Nut Brown-dk.	

Step 2: Backstitch (1 strand)

339		920	Copper-med. (large onions)
246		319	Pistachio Green-vy. dk. (lettuce, green onions)
363		436	Tan (banana, pear)

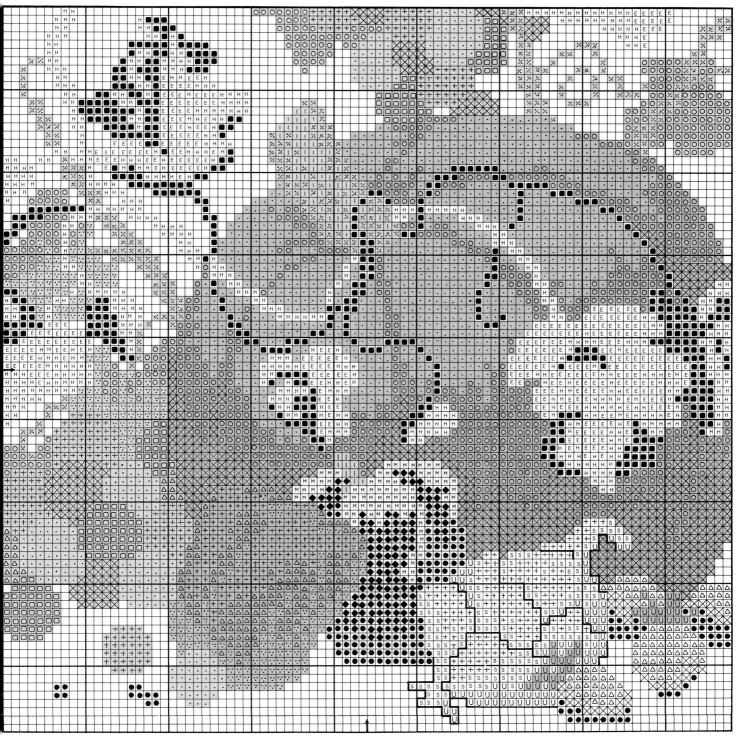

Stitch Count: 88 x 87 (Section B)

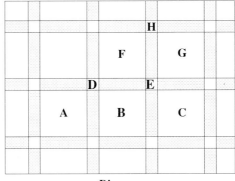

Diagram

Stitch Count: 86 x 83 (Section C)

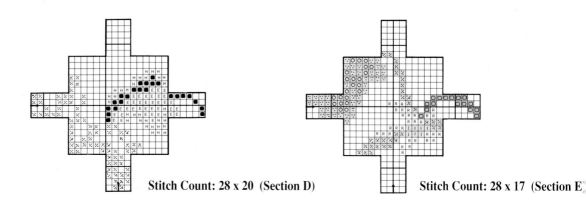

Stitch Count: 28 x 20 (Section D)

Stitch Count: 28 x 17 (Section E)

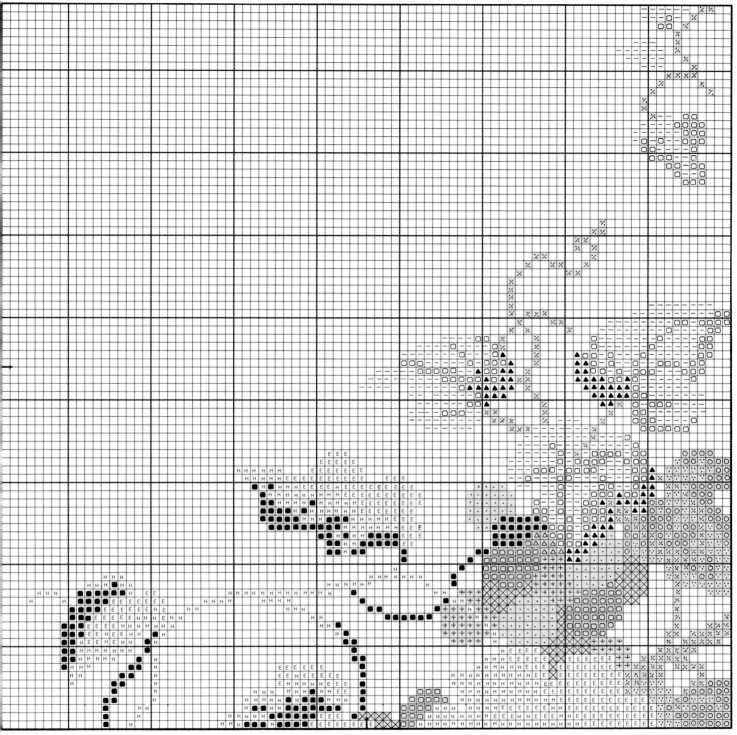

Stitch Count: 85 x 88 (Section F)

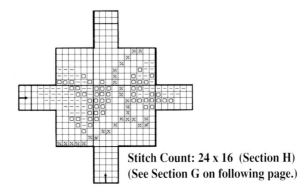

Stitch Count: 24 x 16 (Section H)
(See Section G on following page.)

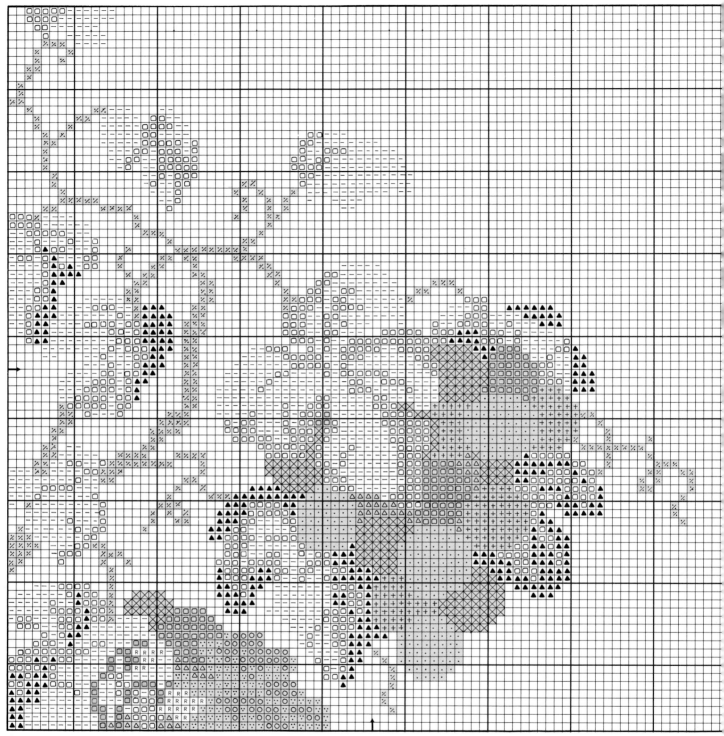

Stitch Count: 83 x 88 (Section G)

**CROCHET
ABBREVIATIONS**

ch—chain
dc—double crochet
rep—repeat
sc—single crochet
sk—skip
sl st—slip stitch
sp(s)—space(s)

Welcome Wreath

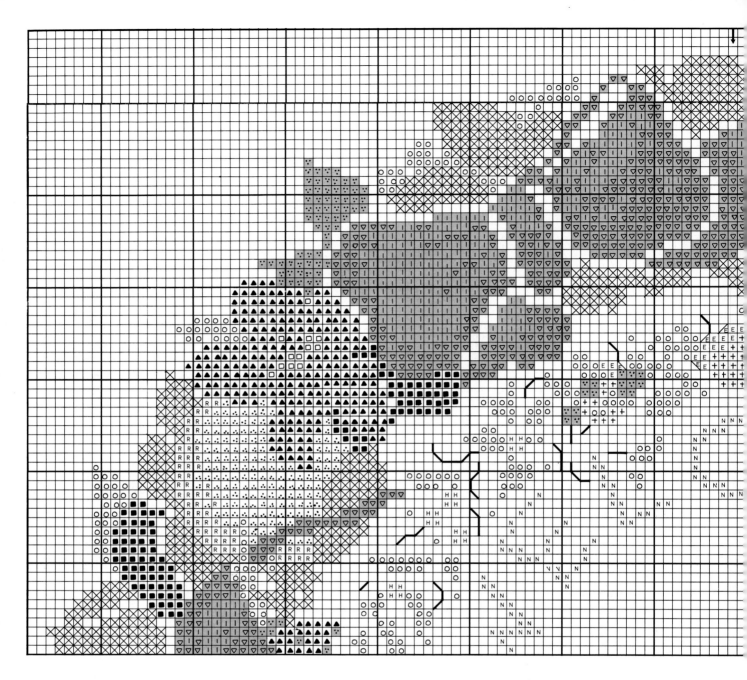

SAMPLE
Stitched on cream Belfast Linen 32 over 2 threads, the finished design size is 9¼" x 9¼". The fabric was cut 16" x 16".

FABRICS	DESIGN SIZES
Aida 11	13½" x 13½"
Aida 14	10⅝" x 10⅝"
Aida 18	8¼" x 8¼"
Hardanger 22	6¾" x 6¾"

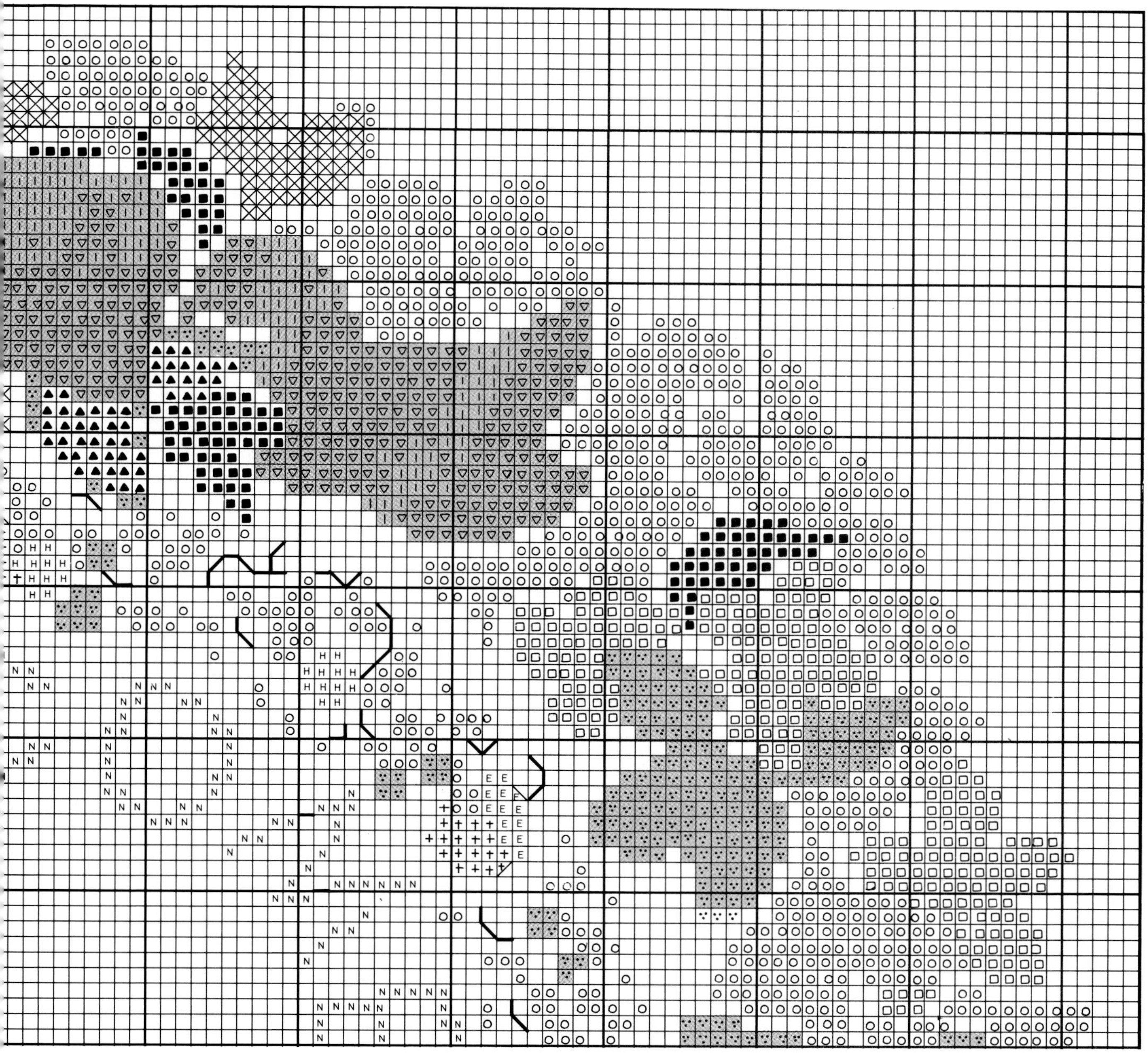

Stitch Count: 149 x 148

Anchor		DMC (used for sample)

Step 1: Cross-stitch (2 strands)

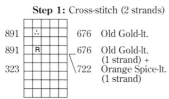

891	∴	676 Old Gold-lt.
891	R	676 Old Gold-lt. (1 strand) +
323	╱	722 Orange Spice-lt. (1 strand)

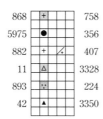

868	+	758 Terra Cotta-lt.
5975	●	356 Terra Cotta-med.
882	+╱	407 Pecan
11	△	3328 Salmon-dk.
893	∴	224 Shell Pink-lt.
42	▲	3350 Dusty Rose-dk.

970	H	315 Antique Mauve-vy. dk.
870	S	3042 Antique Violet-lt.
101	M	327 Antique Violet-vy. dk.
159	□	827 Blue-vy. lt.
161	∴	826 Blue-med.
922	N	930 Antique Blue-dk.

167	I	598	Turquoise-lt.
168	▽	807	Peacock Blue
843	■	3364	Pine Green
875	O	503	Blue Green-med.
878	X	501	Blue Green-dk.
936	E /	632	Pecan-dk.

Step 2: Backstitch (1 strand)

| 922 | 930 | Antique Blue-dk. (in "M") |
| 936 | 632 | Pecan-dk. (stems) |

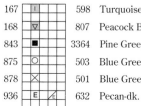

Glorious Nativity

SAMPLE
Stitched on raw Belfast Linen 32 over 2 threads, the finished design size is 7⅝" x 15¾". The fabric was cut 14" x 22".

FABRICS	DESIGN SIZES
Aida 11	11⅛" x 22⅞"
Aida 14	8¾" x 17⅞"
Aida 18	6¾" x 14"
Hardanger 22	5½" x 11⅜"

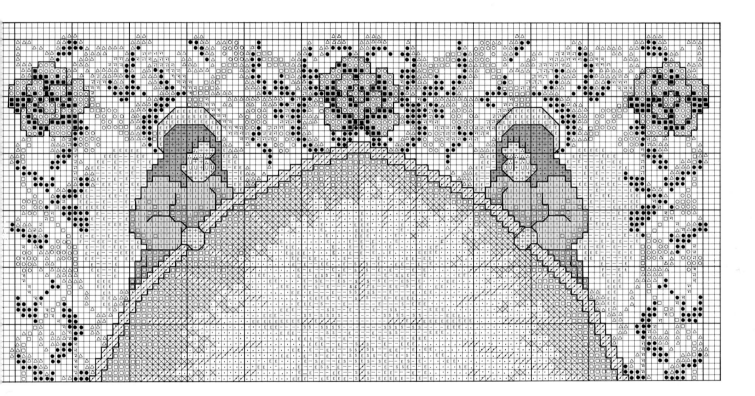

Anchor   DMC (used for sample)

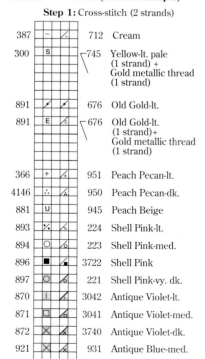

Step 1: Cross-stitch (2 strands)

Anchor	DMC	Name
387	712	Cream
300	745	Yellow-lt. pale (1 strand) + Gold metallic thread (1 strand)
891	676	Old Gold-lt.
891	676	Old Gold-lt. (1 strand)+ Gold metallic thread (1 strand)
366	951	Peach Pecan-lt.
4146	950	Peach Pecan-dk.
881	945	Peach Beige
893	224	Shell Pink-lt.
894	223	Shell Pink-med.
896	3722	Shell Pink
897	221	Shell Pink-vy. dk.
870	3042	Antique Violet-lt.
871	3041	Antique Violet-med.
872	3740	Antique Violet-dk.
921	931	Antique Blue-med.

Anchor	DMC	Name
900	928	Slate Green-lt.
849	927	Slate Green-med.
779	926	Slate Green
875	503	Blue Green-med.
876	502	Blue Green
878	501	Blue Green-dk.
859	3052	Green Gray-med.
846	3051	Green Gray-dk.
956	613	Drab Brown-lt.
898	611	Drab Brown-dk.
887	3045	Yellow Beige-dk.
373	422	Hazel Nut Brown-lt.
373	422	Hazel Nut Brown-lt. (1 strand) +
375	420	Hazel Nut Brown-dk. (1 strand)
375	420	Hazel Nut Brown-dk.
362	437	Tan-lt.
363	436	Tan
370	434	Brown-lt.

Anchor	DMC	Name
376	842	Beige Brown-vy. lt.
378	841	Beige Brown-lt.
379	840	Beige Brown-med.
380	839	Beige Brown-dk.
381	838	Beige Brown-vy. dk.
273	3787	Brown Gray-dk.
397	762	Pearl Gray-vy. lt.

Step 2: Backstitch (1 strand)

Anchor	DMC	Name
897	221	Shell Pink-vy. dk. (flowers, verse)
273	3787	Brown Gray-dk. (all else, except straw)

Step 3: Long Stitch (1 strand)

Anchor	DMC	Name
887	3045	Yellow Beige-dk. (straw)

70

Unto you is born this day in the city of David a Saviour which is Christ the Lord

Stitch Count: 122 x 251

Everyday Pleasures

Everyday pleasures abound in this diverse assortment of designs. Decorate throughout the year with botanical pillows and framed pieces stitched in rich spring and autumn colors. Recapture special memories with a family heirloom floral mat, or add a whimsical touch to a youngster's room with Lewis Carroll's perennially late rabbit.

Family Heirloom

SAMPLE

Stitched on cream Aida 14 over 1 thread, the finished design size is 11¼" x 13¼". The fabric was cut 18" x 20".

FABRICS

FABRICS	DESIGN SIZES
Aida 11	14¼" x 17"
Aida 18	8¾" x 10¼"
Hardanger 22	7¼" x 8½"

MATERIALS

Completed cross-stitch on cream Aida 14
Professionally cut mat (see Step 1)
Dressmaker's pen
Double-sided tape
Masking tape

DIRECTIONS

1. Have a professional framer cut mat board. Outside dimensions are 14½" x 16¾". Window dimensions are 7¼" x 9¼".

2. With design centered, trim Aida to measure 16½" x 18¾".

3. Place Aida wrong side up on flat surface. Center mat over fabric and, using dressmaker's pen, trace edge of window onto fabric. Then draw a smaller window 2" inside first window. Cut along inside traced line. Clip corners between 2 traced lines at a 45° angle.

4. On wrong side of mat, run a strip of double-sided tape along top edge of window. Fold fabric over mat, making sure that violet cross-stitched border is parallel to inside edge of mat.

5. Repeat Step 4 for bottom edge of window and then sides.

6. Still on wrong side of mat, run a strip of double-sided tape along top outside edge to within 2" of corners. Fold fabric over edge, pulling it taut. Repeat along bottom edge and then sides. Trim excess fabric from corners on back and secure with masking tape. Place mat in a ready-made frame or have a professional framer complete framing.

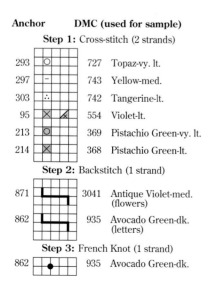

Anchor		DMC (used for sample)	
		Step 1: Cross-stitch (2 strands)	
293	O	727	Topaz-vy. lt.
297	-	743	Yellow-med.
303	∴	742	Tangerine-lt.
95	X	554	Violet-lt.
213	O	369	Pistachio Green-vy. lt.
214	X	368	Pistachio Green-lt.
		Step 2: Backstitch (1 strand)	
871		3041	Antique Violet-med. (flowers)
862		935	Avocado Green-dk. (letters)
		Step 3: French Knot (1 strand)	
862	●	935	Avocado Green-dk.

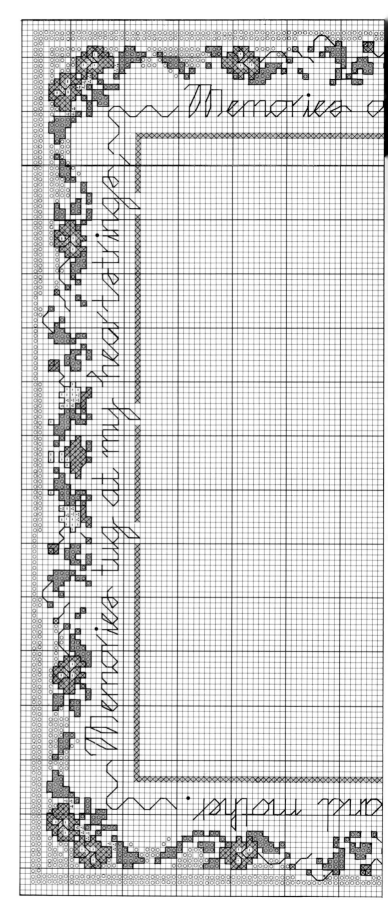

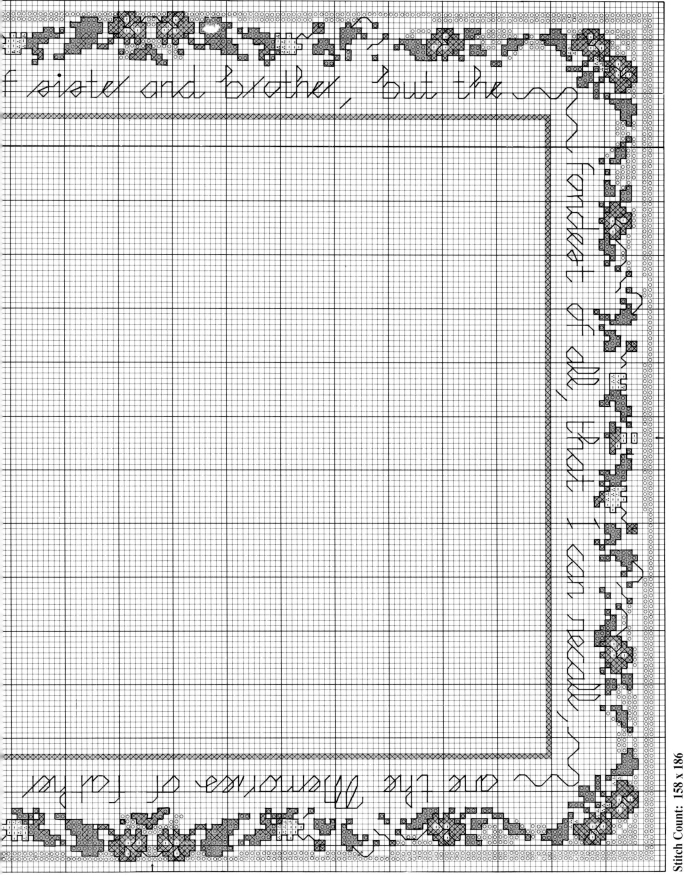

No Time to Spare

SAMPLE
Stitched on white Belfast Linen 32 over 2 threads, the finished design size is 9½" x 4½". The fabric was cut 16" x 11".

FABRICS	DESIGN SIZES
Aida 11	13⅞" x 6⅝"
Aida 14	10⅞" x 5¼"
Aida 18	8½" x 4"
Hardanger 22	6⅞" x 3⅜"

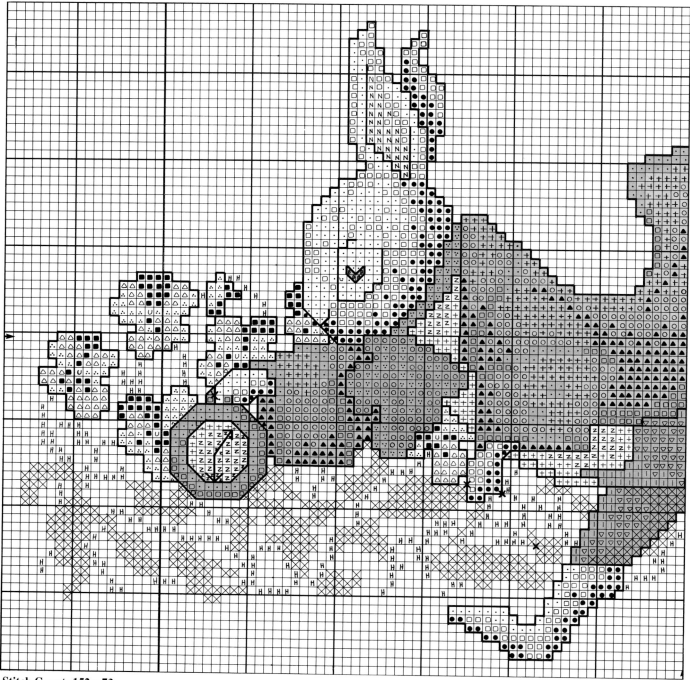

Stitch Count: 152 x 73

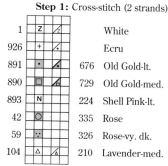

Anchor			DMC (used for sample)	
			Step 1: Cross-stitch (2 strands)	
1	Z	◢		White
926	+	◢		Ecru
891	⦁	◢	676	Old Gold-lt.
890	▢	◢	729	Old Gold-med.
893	N		224	Shell Pink-lt.
42	◎		335	Rose
59	⦂		326	Rose-vy. dk.
104	△	◢	210	Lavender-med.

105	⦂	◢	209	Lavender-dk.
118	■	◢	340	Blue Violet-med.
121	+		793	Cornflower Blue-med.
940	◎	◣	792	Cornflower Blue-dk.
941	▲	◢	791	Cornflower Blue-vy. dk.
858	✕	◢	524	Fern Green-vy. lt.
859	H		522	Fern Green
876	I		502	Blue Green
878	▽		501	Blue Green-dk.

879	✕		500	Blue Green-vy. dk.
885	U		739	Tan-ultra vy. lt.
376	⦁	◢	842	Beige Brown-vy. lt.
378	▢		841	Beige Brown-lt.
379	●	◢	840	Beige Brown-med.
380		◢	839	Beige Brown-dk.

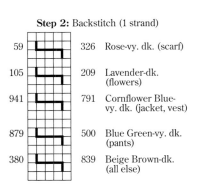

Floral Tapestry Trio

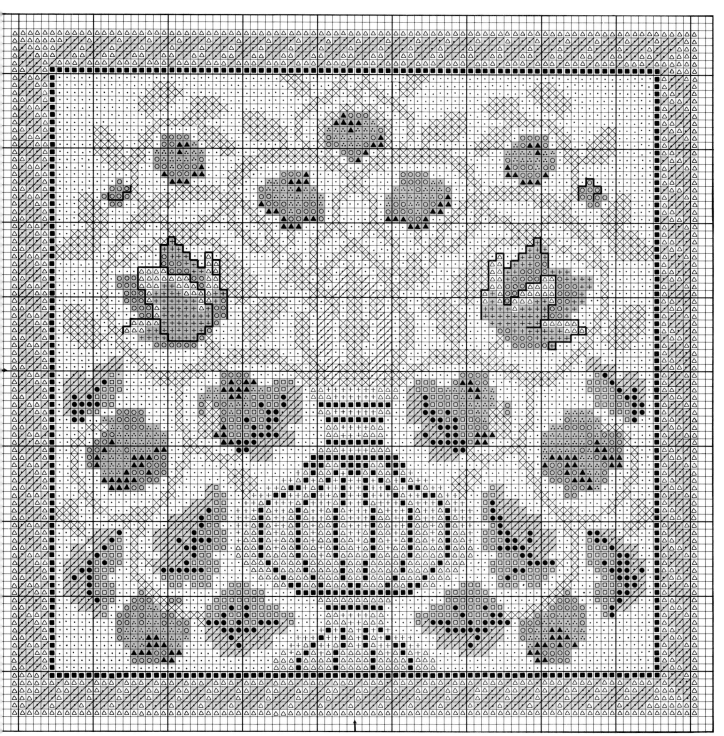

Stitch Count: 92 x 92 (Design 1)

Stitch Count: 93 x 93 (Design 2)

titch Count: 92 x 92 (Design 3)

SAMPLE for Design 1

Stitched on cream Aida 11 over 1 thread, the finished design size is 8⅜" x 8⅜". The fabric was cut 12" x 12". *Note:* Four strands of DMC floss equal 2 strands of Medicis wool.

FABRICS	DESIGN SIZES
Aida 14	6⅝" x 6⅝"
Aida 18	5⅛" x 5⅛"
Hardanger 22	4⅛" x 4⅛"

SAMPLE for Design 2

Stitched on cream Aida 11 over 1 thread, the finished design size 8½" x 8½". The fabric was cut 12" x 12". *Note:* Four strands of DMC floss equal 2 strands of Medicis wool.

FABRICS	DESIGN SIZES
Aida 14	6⅝" x 6⅝"
Aida 18	5⅛" x 5⅛"
Hardanger 22	4¼" x 4¼"

SAMPLE for Design 3

Stitched on cream Aida 11 over 1 thread, the finished design size is 8⅜" x 8⅜". The fabric was cut 12" x 12". *Note:* Four strands of DMC floss equal 2 strands of Medicis wool.

FABRICS	DESIGN SIZES
Aida 14	6⅝" x 6⅝"
Aida 18	5⅛" x 5⅛"
Hardanger 22	4⅛" x 4⅛"

Design 1

DMC — **Medicis Wool (used for sample)**

Step 1: Cross-stitch (2 strands)

DMC		Medicis Wool	
746	+	8328	Off White
676	△	8314	Old Gold-lt.
422	■	8322	Hazel Nut Brown-lt.
963	⋰	8132	Wild Rose-vy. lt.
754	+	8139	Peach-lt.
224	O	8113	Shell Pink-lt.
223	▲	8107	Shell Pink-med.
3053	✕	8405	Green Gray
470	╱	8412	Avocado Green-lt.
367	□	8406	Pistachio Green-dk.
502	●	8407	Blue Green
500	·	8415	Blue Green-vy. dk.

Step 2: Backstitch (1 strand)

356		**DMC Floss** 356 Terra Cotta-med.

Design 2

DMC — **Medicis Wool (used for sample)**

Step 1: Cross-stitch (2 strands)

DMC		Medicis Wool	
676	I	8314	Old Gold-lt.
422	⋰	8322	Hazel Nut Brown-lt.
963	B	8132	Wild Rose-vy. lt.
754	▫	8139	Peach-lt.
224	+	8113	Shell Pink-lt.
223	●	8107	Shell Pink-med.
315	U	8122	Antique Mauve-vy. dk.
800	∴	8800	Delft-pale
3348	△	8420	Yellow Green-lt.
3053	E	8405	Green Gray
470	▲	8412	Avocado Green-lt.
367	O	8406	Pistachio Green-dk.
319	□	8414	Pistachio Green-vy. dk.
502	■	8407	Blue Green
500	✕	8415	Blue Green-vy. dk.
3032	╱	8307	Mocha Brown-med.

Step 2: Backstitch (1 strand)

356		**DMC Floss** 356 Terra Cotta-med.

Design 3

DMC — **Medicis Wool (used for sample)**

Step 1: Cross-stitch (2 strands)

DMC		Medicis Wool	
676	I	8314	Old Gold-lt.
422	□	8322	Hazel Nut Brown-lt.
754	△	8139	Peach-lt.
224	⋰	8113	Shell Pink-lt.
223	■	8107	Shell Pink-med.
3768	∴	8203	Slate Green-dk.
470	✕	8412	Avocado Green-lt.
319	●	8414	Pistachio Green-vy. dk.
500	╱	8415	Blue Green-vy. dk.
3011	O	8309	Khaki Green-dk.

Step 2: Backstitch (1 strand)

356		**DMC Floss** 356 Terra Cotta-med.

MATERIALS (for 1 pillow)
Completed cross-stitch on cream Aida 11
¼ yard of coordinating fabric for back; matching thread
⅜ yard of contrasting fabric for corded piping; matching thread
⅓ yard of medium cording
Stuffing

DIRECTIONS
All seam allowances are ¼".

1. Trim design piece (pillow front) to ¼" outside all edges of design. Using pillow front as a pattern, cut pillow back from coordinating fabric. From contrasting fabric, cut 1½"-wide bias strips, piecing as needed to equal 36". With bias strip and cording, make 36" of corded piping.

2. With right sides facing and raw edges aligned, stitch piping around pillow front, stitching close to edges of stitched design. With right sides facing and raw edges aligned, stitch pillow front to pillow back, sewing along stitching line of piping and leaving an opening for turning. Trim corners and turn. Stuff firmly. Slipstitch opening closed.

Birds and Flowers

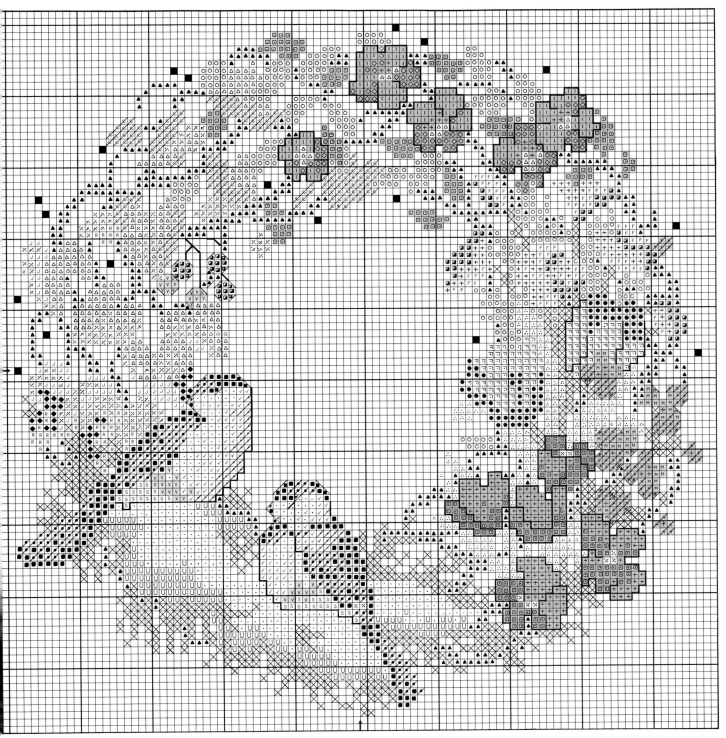

Stitch Count: 96 x 97

SAMPLE

Stitched on cream Belfast Linen 32 over 2 threads, the finished design size is 6" x 6". The fabric was cut 12" x 12". See Suppliers for Mill Hill Beads.

FABRICS

Aida 11
Aida 14
Aida 18
Hardanger 22

DESIGN SIZES

8¾" x 8⅞"
6⅞" x 6⅞"
5⅜" x 5⅜"
4⅜" x 4⅜"

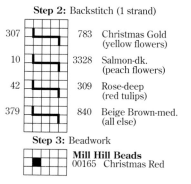

Anchor	DMC (used for sample)	

Step 1: Cross-stitch (2 strands)

Anchor		DMC	
1			White
293		727	Topaz-vy. lt.
295		726	Topaz-lt.
306		725	Topaz
307		783	Christmas Gold
901		680	Old Gold-dk.
6		353	Peach
9575		760	Salmon
10		3328	Salmon-dk.
13		347	Salmon-vy. dk.
8		352	Coral-lt.
9		351	Coral
11		350	Coral-med.
76		961	Wild Rose-dk.
42		309	Rose-deep
98		553	Violet-med.
101		327	Antique Violet-vy. dk.
128		800	Delft-pale
874		833	Olive Green-lt.
266		3347	Yellow Green-med.
244		987	Forest Green-dk.
215		320	Pistachio Green-med.
246		319	Pistachio Green-vy. dk.
307		977	Golden Brown-lt.
308		976	Golden Brown-med.
387		822	Beige Gray-lt.
830		644	Beige Gray-med.
379		840	Beige Brown-med.
381		838	Beige Brown-vy. dk.
382		3371	Black Brown

Step 2: Backstitch (1 strand)

Anchor		DMC	
307		783	Christmas Gold (yellow flowers)
10		3328	Salmon-dk. (peach flowers)
42		309	Rose-deep (red tulips)
379		840	Beige Brown-med. (all else)

Step 3: Beadwork

Mill Hill Beads
00165 Christmas Red

Autumn Beauty

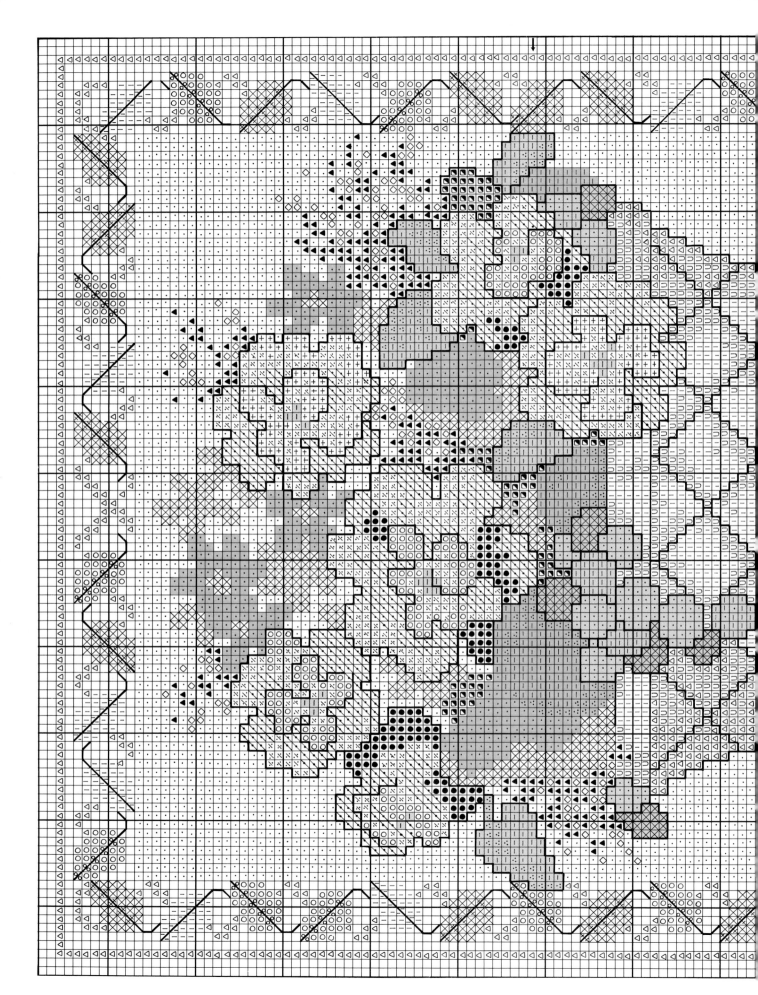

Stitch Count: 104 x 111

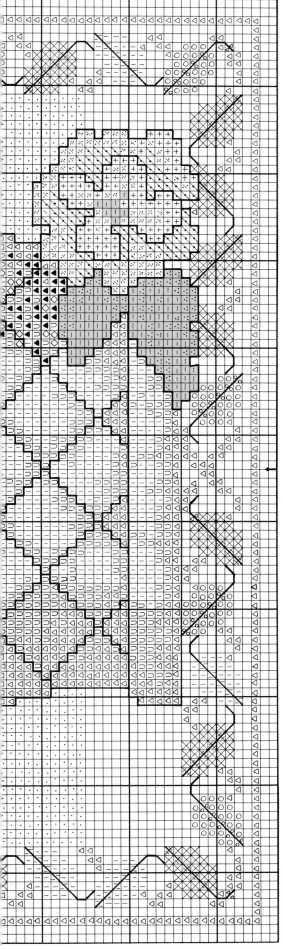

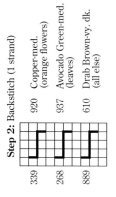

SAMPLE

Stitched on raw Belfast Linen 32 over 2 threads, the finished design size is 6½" x 7". The fabric was cut 13" x 13".

FABRICS — DESIGN SIZES

FABRICS	DESIGN SIZES
Aida 11	9½" x 10⅛"
Aida 14	7⅜" x 7⅞"
Aida 18	5¾" x 6⅛"
Hardanger 22	4¾" x 5"

Step 1: Cross-stitch (2 strands)

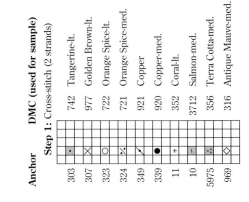

Anchor		DMC (used for sample)	
303	·	742	Tangerine-lt.
307	X	977	Golden Brown-lt.
323	O	722	Orange Spice-lt.
324	✗	721	Orange Spice-med.
349	↗	921	Copper
339	●	920	Copper-med.
11	+	352	Coral-lt.
10	–	3712	Salmon-med.
5975	▦	356	Terra Cotta-med.
969	◇	316	Antique Mauve-med.

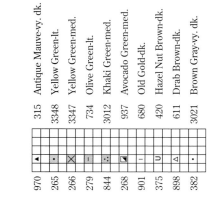

Anchor		DMC	
970	◀	315	Antique Mauve-vy. dk.
265	·	3348	Yellow Green-lt.
266	X	3347	Yellow Green-med.
279	–	734	Olive Green-lt.
844	∴	3012	Khaki Green-med.
268	◪	937	Avocado Green-med.
901	–	680	Old Gold-dk.
375	U	420	Hazel Nut Brown-dk.
898	△	611	Drab Brown-dk.
382	·	3021	Brown Gray-vy. dk.

Step 2: Backstitch (1 strand)

Anchor	DMC	
339	920	Copper-med. (orange flowers)
268	937	Avocado Green-med. (leaves)
889	610	Drab Brown-vy. dk. (all else)

Christmas Towels

SAMPLE for Towels

Stitched on deep teal or rich cranberry Christmas Fingertip Towel 14 over 1 thread. For each towel, stitch 2 side sections and 1 center section. See Suppliers for towels.

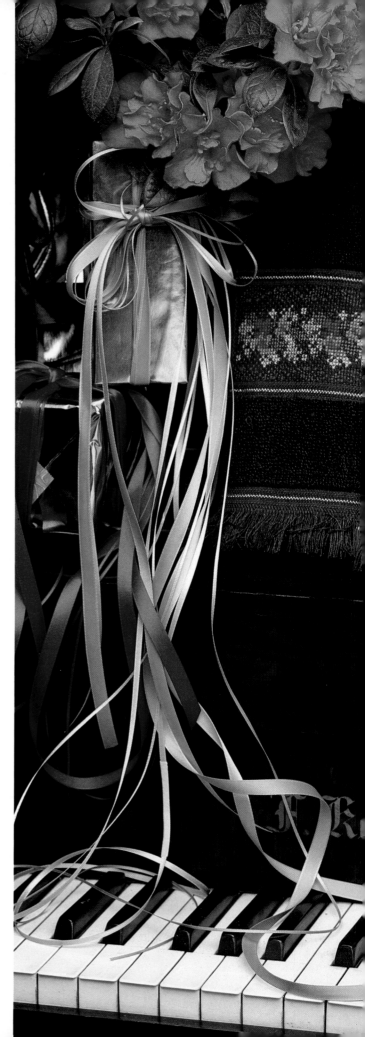

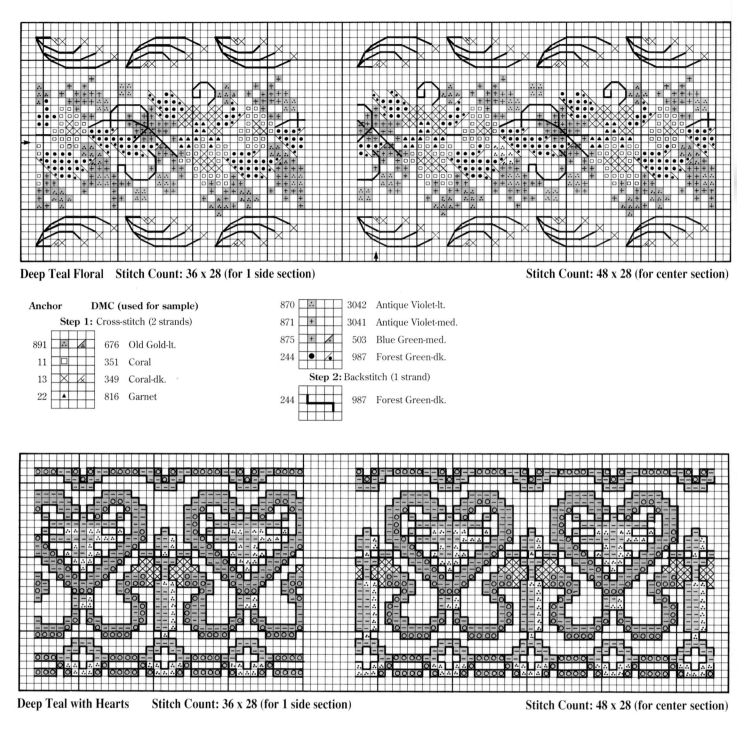

Deep Teal Floral   Stitch Count: 36 x 28 (for 1 side section)

Stitch Count: 48 x 28 (for center section)

Anchor		DMC (used for sample)	
	Step 1: Cross-stitch (2 strands)		
891		676	Old Gold-lt.
11		351	Coral
13		349	Coral-dk.
22		816	Garnet

870		3042	Antique Violet-lt.
871		3041	Antique Violet-med.
875		503	Blue Green-med.
244		987	Forest Green-dk.
	Step 2: Backstitch (1 strand)		
244		987	Forest Green-dk.

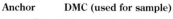

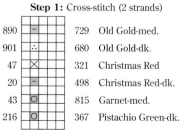

Deep Teal with Hearts   Stitch Count: 36 x 28 (for 1 side section)

Stitch Count: 48 x 28 (for center section)

Anchor		DMC (used for sample)	
	Step 1: Cross-stitch (2 strands)		
890	–	729	Old Gold-med.
901		680	Old Gold-dk.
47	×	321	Christmas Red
20	–	498	Christmas Red-dk.
43	○	815	Garnet-med.
216	○	367	Pistachio Green-dk.

	Step 2: Backstitch (1 strand)	
		Gold metallic thread

94

Deep Teal Fleur-de-lis   Stitch Count: 36 x 28 (for 1 side section)   Stitch Count: 48 x 28 (for center section)

Anchor	DMC (used for sample)

Step 1: Cross-stitch (2 strands)

Step 2: Backstitch (1 strand)

Gold metallic thread

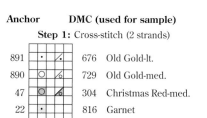

891	676 Old Gold-lt.
890	729 Old Gold-med.
47	304 Christmas Red-med.
22	816 Garnet

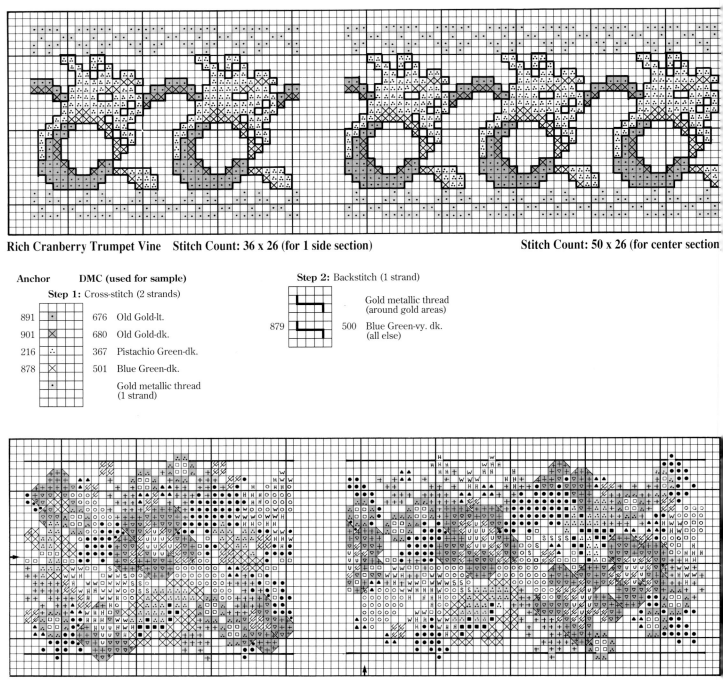

Rich Cranberry Trumpet Vine   Stitch Count: 36 x 26 (for 1 side section)

Stitch Count: 50 x 26 (for center section)

Anchor		DMC (used for sample)

Step 1: Cross-stitch (2 strands)

Anchor		DMC	
891	·	676	Old Gold-lt.
901	X	680	Old Gold-dk.
216	∴	367	Pistachio Green-dk.
878	X	501	Blue Green-dk.
	·		Gold metallic thread (1 strand)

Step 2: Backstitch (1 strand)

Gold metallic thread (around gold areas)

879		500	Blue Green-vy. dk. (all else)

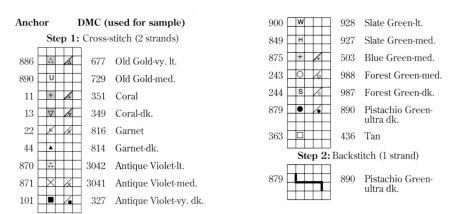

Rich Cranberry Floral   Stitch Count: 36 x 28 (for 1 side section)

Stitch Count: 48 x 28 (for center section)

Anchor		DMC (used for sample)

Step 1: Cross-stitch (2 strands)

Anchor		DMC	
886	∴	677	Old Gold-vy. lt.
890	U	729	Old Gold-med.
11	+	351	Coral
13	▽	349	Coral-dk.
22		816	Garnet
44	▲	814	Garnet-dk.
870	∴	3042	Antique Violet-lt.
871	X	3041	Antique Violet-med.
101	■	327	Antique Violet-vy. dk.

Anchor		DMC	
900	W	928	Slate Green-lt.
849	H	927	Slate Green-med.
875	+	503	Blue Green-med.
243	O	988	Forest Green-med.
244	S	987	Forest Green-dk.
879	●	890	Pistachio Green-ultra dk.
363	□	436	Tan

Step 2: Backstitch (1 strand)

879		890	Pistachio Green-ultra dk.

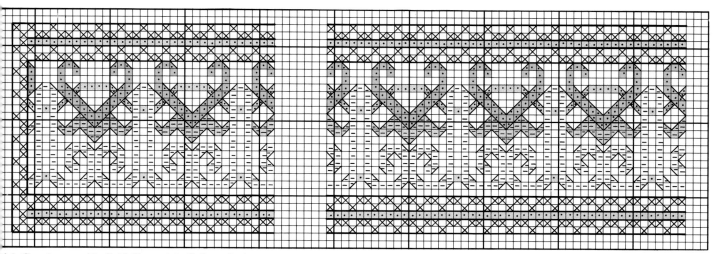

Rich Cranberry with Gold Geometric (left section)

(center section)

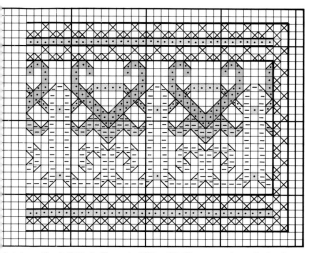

(right section) Stitch Count: 132 x 28 (for complete design)

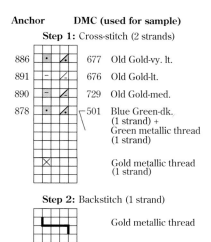

Anchor				DMC	(used for sample)

Step 1: Cross-stitch (2 strands)

886				677	Old Gold-vy. lt.
891				676	Old Gold-lt.
890				729	Old Gold-med.
878				501	Blue Green-dk. (1 strand) + Green metallic thread (1 strand)
					Gold metallic thread (1 strand)

Step 2: Backstitch (1 strand)

Gold metallic thread

97

Capture The Holiday Spirit

The holiday spirit is yours to keep — and to share — when you focus on these four popular holidays. First, dress up your home with pillows: Bright spring flowers spell out "Happy Easter," and flags from the early years of our nation mark Independence Day. A Halloween windsock will add a bewitching chill to the air. And together for the first time are all seven of our beloved Father Christmases.

Happy Easter

Stitch Count: 155 x 95

Anchor		DMC (used for sample)
Step 1: Cross-stitch (2 strands)		
1		White
386		746 Off White
301	U	744 Yellow-pale
303		742 Tangerine-lt.
891	M	676 Old Gold-lt.
329		3340 Apricot-med.
25	I	3708 Melon-lt.
26		894 Carnation-vy. lt.
35	H	891 Carnation-dk.
35	J	891 Carnation-dk. (1 strand) +
329		3340 Apricot-med. (1 strand)
59	▲	326 Rose-vy. dk.

76	⊠	603	Cranberry
85	G	3609	Plum-ultra lt.
88	+	718	Plum
69	○	3687	Mauve
70		3685	Mauve-dk.
95	N	554	Violet-lt.
98	△	553	Violet-med.
117	R	341	Blue Violet-lt.
119	■	333	Blue Violet-dk.
900	−	928	Slate Green-lt.
849	B	927	Slate Green-med.
265	S	3348	Yellow Green-lt.
266	□	3347	Yellow Green-med.
216	⊠	367	Pistachio Green-dk.
209	○	913	Nile Green-med.

228		910	Emerald Green-dk.
187	▽	992	Aquamarine
189	●	991	Aquamarine-dk.

Step 2: Backstitch (1 strand)

901		680	Old Gold-dk. (daffodils)
69		3687	Mauve (tulips)
921		931	Antique Blue-med. (lilies, sweet peas)
216		367	Pistachio Green-dk. (all else)

Step 3: Smyrna Cross-stitch (1 strand)

921	✳	931	Antique Blue-med.

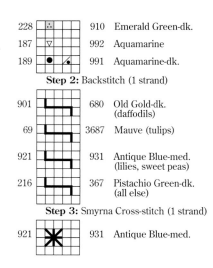

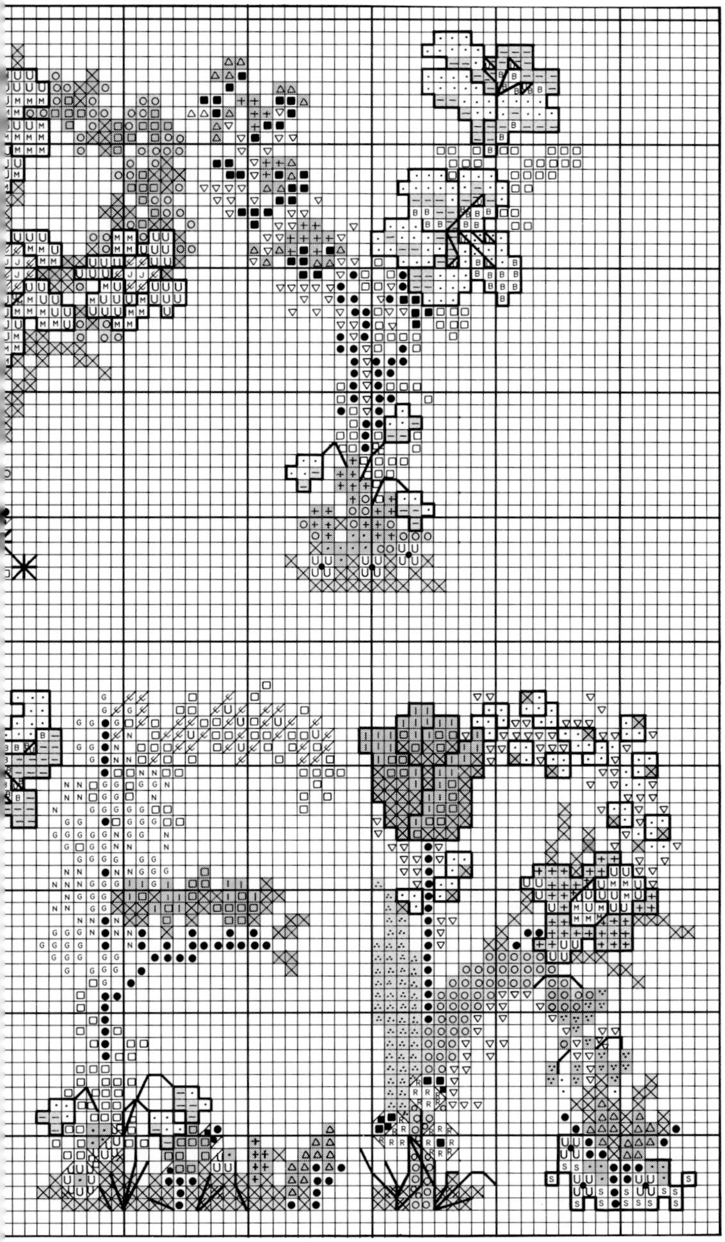

Step 4: French Knot (1 strand)

216 ● 367 Pistachio Green-dk.

SAMPLE

Stitched on moss green Lugana 25 over 2 threads, the finished design size is 12⅜" x 7⅝". The fabric was cut 20" x 14".

FABRICS	DESIGN SIZES
Aida 11	14⅛" x 8⅝"
Aida 14	11⅛" x 6¾"
Aida 18	8⅝" x 5¼"
Hardanger 22	7" x 4⅜"

MATERIALS

Completed cross-stitch on moss green Lugana 25; matching thread
½ yard of unstitched moss green Lugana 25 for pillow back
1¼ yards of print fabric
4 yards (¼"-diameter) cording
½ yard of fleece
Stuffing

DIRECTIONS

All seam allowances are ¼".

1. With design centered, trim Lugana to 17" x 13". From remaining Lugana, cut a 17" x 13" piece for pillow back. From fleece, cut 2 (17" x 13") pieces. Pin fleece to wrong side of front and back pieces. Zigzag edges together. Press as needed to keep smooth.

2. To make corded piping and tubing, cut 1"-wide bias strips from printed fabric, piecing as needed to equal 4 yards. Make 60" of corded piping and 83" of corded tubing. Cut tubing into 1 (35") piece and 4 (12") pieces.

3. With right sides facing and raw edges aligned, stitch piping to right side of design piece. With right sides facing, stitch design piece to pillow back on stitching line of piping, leaving an opening for turning. Clip corners. Turn.

4. To make loops on top edge of pillow, mark center of 35" piece of corded tubing. Make a 2½" loop. Slipstitch loop to center top of pillow. Working to the right, make 3 more loops, decreasing in size and ending 5½" from corner. Slipstitch in place. Repeat for 3 loops on left side.

5. Stuff pillow firmly. Slipstitch opening closed.

6. For corner bow, use 1 (12") piece of corded tubing. Make 1½" loops (see Diagram). Tack loops securely. Repeat to make 3 more bows. Slipstitch a bow to each corner.

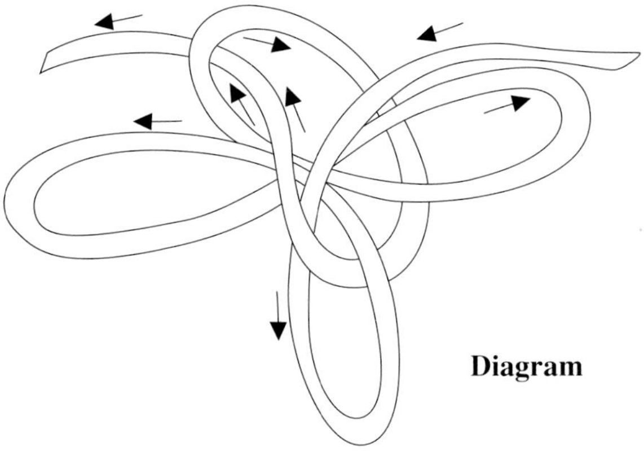

Diagram

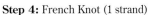

Patriotic Pillows

SAMPLE for Liberty Flag Pillow
Stitched on natural Dirty Linen 26 over 2 threads, the finished design size is 9¼" x 6⅞". The fabric was cut 16" x 13".

FABRICS	DESIGN SIZES
Aida 11	11" x 8⅛"
Aida 14	8⅝" x 6⅜"
Aida 18	6¾" x 5"
Hardanger 22	5½" x 4"

SAMPLE for Stars and Stripes Pillow
Stitched on natural Dirty Linen 26 over 2 threads, the finished design size is 9½" x 7". The fabric was cut 16" x 13".

FABRICS	DESIGN SIZES
Aida 11	11⅛" x 8¼"
Aida 14	8¾" x 6½"
Aida 18	6⅞" x 5"
Hardanger 22	5⅝" x 4⅛"

SAMPLE for Confederate Pillow
Stitched on natural Dirty Linen 26 over 2 threads, the finished design size is 9½" x 7". The fabric was cut 16" x 13".

FABRICS	DESIGN SIZES
Aida 11	11⅛" x 8¼"
Aida 14	8¾" x 6½"
Aida 18	6⅞" x 5"
Hardanger 22	5⅝" x 4⅛"

MATERIALS (for 1 pillow)
Completed cross-stitch on natural Dirty Linen 26
1 yard (45"-wide) bronze satin fabric; matching thread
1½ yards (¼"-diameter) cording
½ yard of fleece
Stuffing

DIRECTIONS
All seam allowances are ¼".

1. With design centered, trim linen to 11" x 8½". From fleece, cut 2 (15½" x 12½") pieces. From satin fabric, cut 1 (15½" x 12½") piece for pillow back, 2 (16" x 3") pieces for top and bottom borders, and 2 (13" x 3") pieces for side borders. Also, from satin fabric, cut 1¼"-wide bias strips, piecing as needed to equal 1½ yards. With bias strips and cording, make corded piping.

2. Mark center of each edge of design piece and 1 long edge of each border strip. With right sides facing, center marks matching, and raw edges aligned, stitch 1 border strip to design piece. Stitch to within ¼" of each corner; backstitch. Repeat to join remaining border strips. Press seams toward borders.

3. To miter corners, fold right sides of 2 adjacent border strips together and stitch at a 45° angle (see Diagram). Trim seam allowance to ¼". Repeat for remaining corners.

4. Pin fleece to wrong side of front and back pieces. Zigzag edges together. Press as needed to keep smooth.

5. With right sides facing and raw edges aligned, stitch piping to pillow front. With right sides facing, stitch pillow front to back, sewing on stitching line of piping and leaving an opening for turning. Clip corners and turn. Stuff pillow firmly. Slipstitch opening closed.

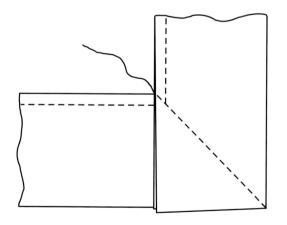

Diagram

Liberty Flag Pillow

Anchor		DMC	(used for sample)
Step 1: Cross-stitch (2 strands)			
885		739	Tan-ultra vy. lt.
887		3046	Yellow Beige-med.
373		3045	Yellow Beige-dk.
13		347	Salmon-vy. dk.
922		930	Antique Blue-dk.
861		3363	Pine Green-med.
Step 2: Backstitch (1 strand)			
885		739	Tan-ultra vy. lt. (stars)
149		311	Navy Blue-med. (lettering, flag outlines)
861		3363	Pine Green-med. (tree trunk)

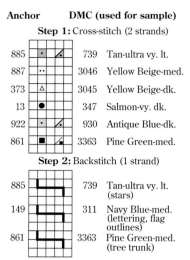

Stars and Stripes Pillow

Anchor		DMC	(used for sample)
Step 1: Cross-stitch (2 strands)			
885		739	Tan-ultra vy. lt.
887		3046	Yellow Beige-med.
373		3045	Yellow Beige-dk.
13		347	Salmon-vy. dk.
920		932	Antique Blue-lt.
922		930	Antique Blue-dk.
Step 2: Backstitch (1 strand)			
885		739	Tan-ultra vy. lt. (star circle, tan lettering)
149		311	Navy Blue-med. (all else)

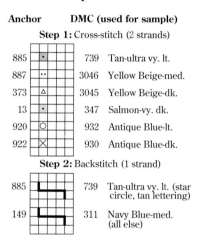

Confederate Pillow

Anchor		DMC	(used for sample)
Step 1: Cross-stitch (2 strands)			
885		739	Tan-ultra vy. lt.
887		3046	Yellow Beige-med.
373		3045	Yellow Beige-dk.
13		347	Salmon-vy. dk.
922		930	Antique Blue-dk.
889		610	Drab Brown-vy. dk.
Step 2: Backstitch (1 strand)			
885		739	Tan-ultra vy. lt. (2 strands) (stars)
149		311	Navy Blue-med. (all else)

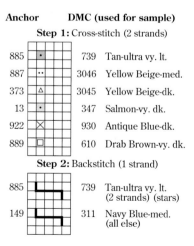

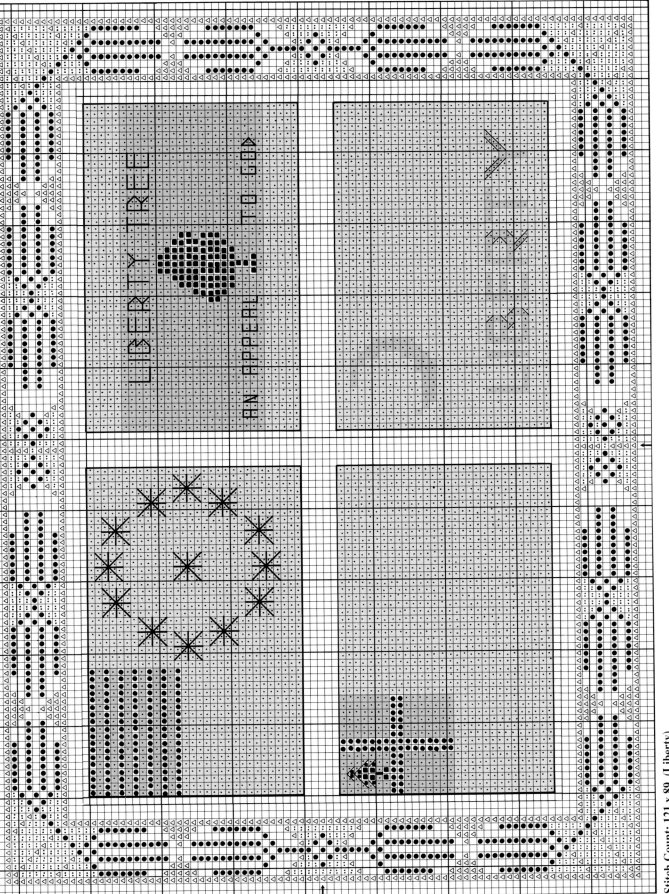

Stitch Count: 121 x 89 (Liberty)

Stitch Count: 123 x 91 (Stars and Stripes)

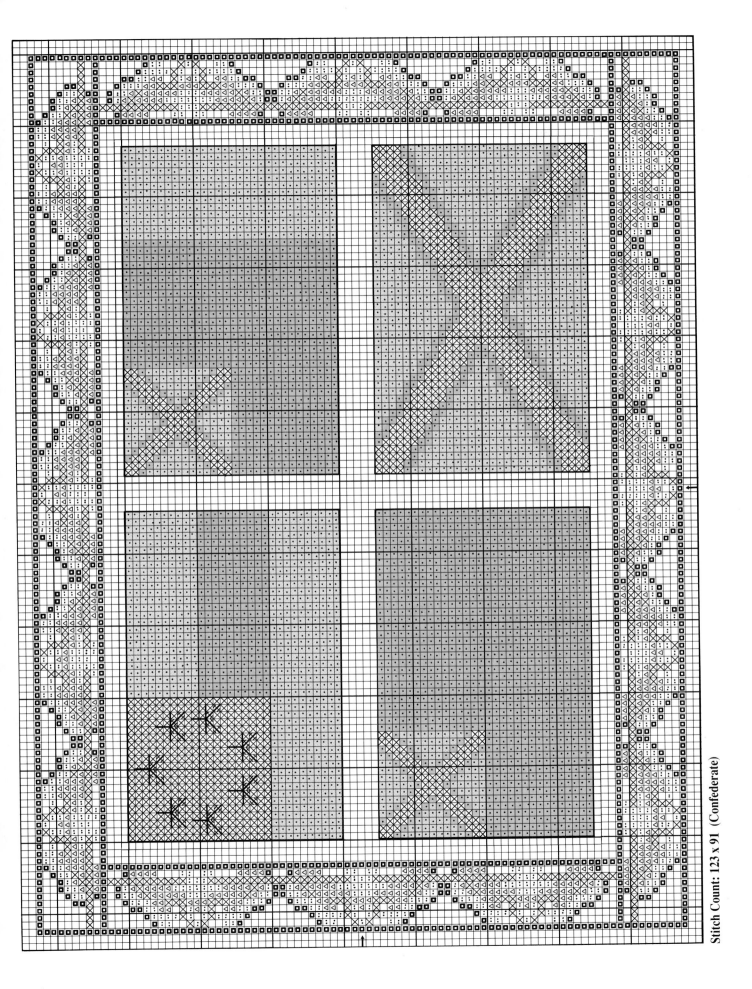

Stitch Count: 123 x 91 (Confederate)

107

Bewitching Windsock

SAMPLE

Stitched on Waste Canvas 10, the finished design size is 5⅛" x 7⅝". The canvas was cut 7" x 10". The fabric was cut 15" x 22".

FABRICS	DESIGN SIZES
Aida 11	4⅝" x 6⅞"
Aida 14	3⅝" x 5½"
Aida 18	2⅞" x 4¼"
Hardanger 22	2⅜" x 3½"

MATERIALS

Completed cross-stitch on green waterproof rip-stop fabric; matching thread
1½ yards of black waterproof rip-stop fabric; matching thread
⅝ yard (1"-wide) belting
5 yards (⅛"-wide) black satin ribbon
White dressmaker's pencil

DIRECTIONS

All seam allowances are ½".

1. With design centered, trim design piece to 14" x 21½". From black fabric, cut 1 (17¼" x 21½") piece for hat; cut 1 (6" x 43") strip for hat ruffle; cut 1 (11" x 43") strip for collar ruffle; and cut 11 (2¾" x 30") strips for streamers.

2. With right sides facing, stitch the 14" edges of design piece together to make a tube. Trim seam to ¼". Repeat with hat piece, stitching the 17¼" edges together. Finish top edge of hat by folding ¼" to wrong side and stitching.

3. Overlap ends of belting 1" and stitch together. Place belting on wrong side at top of hat. Fold top hemmed edge of hat over belting. Stitch hemmed edge to hat, making a 1½" casing.

4. To make hat ruffle, with wrong sides facing, fold 6" x 43" strip in half lengthwise. Stitch ends together to make a circle. Stitch 2 rows of gathering stitches, ¼" apart, around long raw edge of ruffle. Gather ruffle to fit hat bottom. With raw edges aligned and ruffle seam aligned with center back hat seam, stitch ruffle to right side of hat bottom.

5. With right sides facing, raw edges and seams aligned, and ruffle sandwiched between, stitch top of green tube to bottom of hat, sewing on ruffle stitching line. Stitch again, ¼" from edge.

6. To make collar ruffle, follow instructions in Step 4 to gather 11" x 43" strip and attach to green tube bottom.

7. To make streamers, cut 1 end of each 2¾" x 30" strip to a point. Finish long edges and points by turning under ¼" and stitching a narrow hem. With raw edges aligned, pin straight edge of streamers over collar ruffle, overlapping ¼" on each side and adjusting as needed to fit around bottom edge of green tube. Stitch streamers to tube, sewing on ruffle stitching line. Stitch again, ¼" from edge.

8. For hanger, with white pencil, mark 4 points (2 on front, 2 on back), about 3½" in from each side on wrong side at top of hat, just above stitching line of casing. Cut 4 (45") lengths of ribbon. Machine-tack 1 end of 1 ribbon securely to each mark. Knot free ends together.

Anchor		DMC (used for sample)	
Step 1: Cross-stitch (6 strands)			
306		725	Topaz
307		977	Golden Brown-lt.
308		976	Golden Brown-med.
355		975	Golden Brown-dk.
349		921	Copper
874		834	Olive Green-vy. lt.
889		831	Olive Green-med.
906		829	Olive Green-vy. dk.
862		520	Fern Green-dk.
370		434	Brown-lt.
8581		3023	Brown Gray-lt.
403		310	Black
Step 2: Backstitch (2 strands)			
403		310	Black

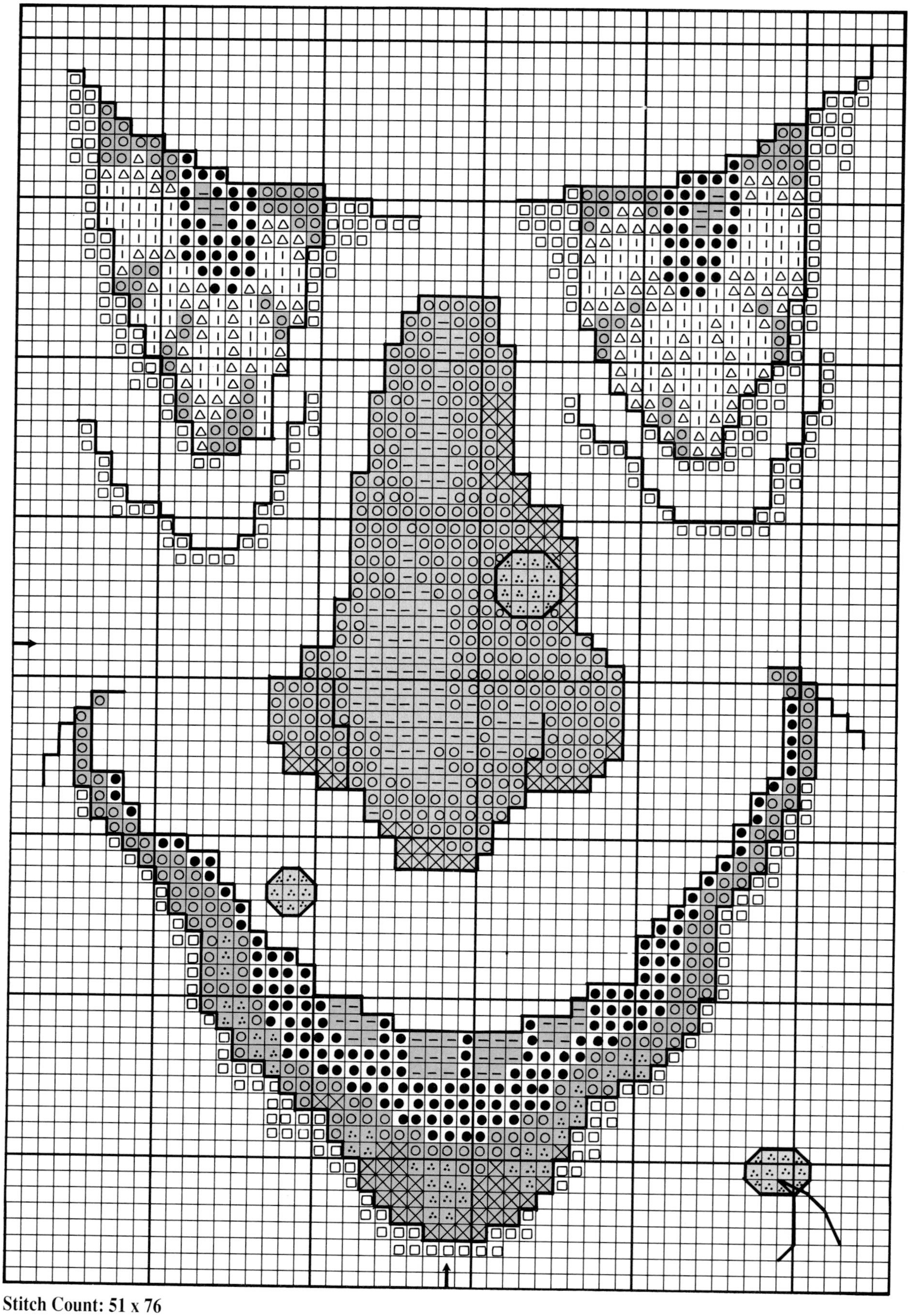

Stitch Count: 51 x 76

Kris Kringle

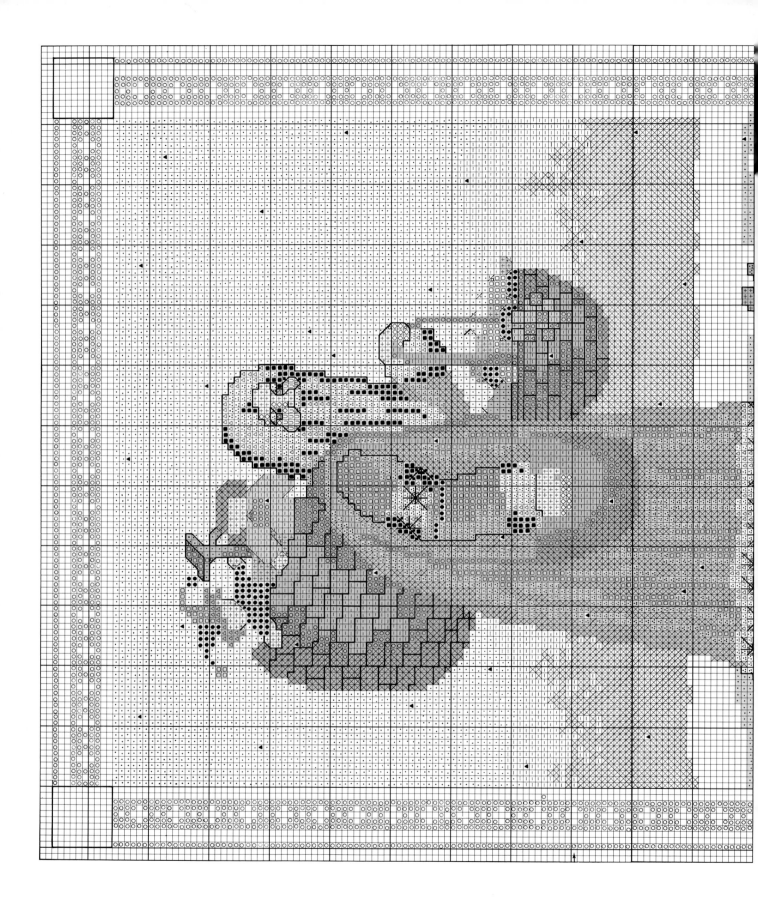

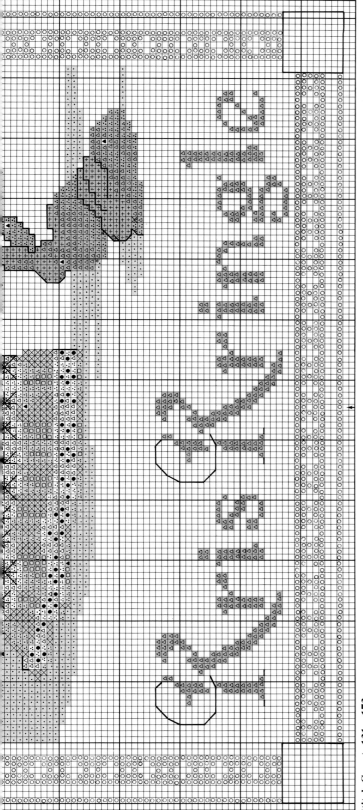

Stitch Count: 131 x 173

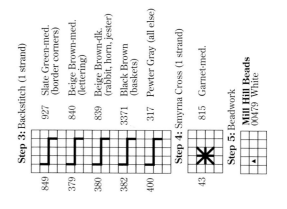

SAMPLE

Stitched on white Belfast Linen 32 over 2
threads, the finished design size is 8¼" x 10¾".
The fabric was cut 15" x 17". See Suppliers
for Mill Hill beads.

FABRICS   **DESIGN SIZES**
Aida 11   11⅞" x 15¾"
Aida 14   9⅜" x 12⅜"
Aida 18   7¼" x 9⅝"
Hardanger 22 6" x 7⅞"

Anchor   **DMC (used for sample)**

Step 1: Cross-stitch (2 strands)

1	White
880	948 Peach-vy. lt.
4146	754 Peach-lt.
366	950 Peach Pecan-dk.
306	725 Topaz
307	783 Christmas Gold
43	815 Garnet-med.
72	902 Garnet-vy. dk.
101	327 Antique Violet-vy. dk.
160	813 Blue-lt.
900	928 Slate Green-lt.
849	927 Slate Green-med.
851	924 Slate Green-vy. dk.
876	502 Blue Green

878	501 Blue Green-dk.
879	500 Blue Green-vy. dk.
307	977 Golden Brown-lt.
378	841 Beige Brown-lt.
379	840 Beige Brown-med.
380	839 Beige Brown-dk.
375	420 Hazel Nut Brown-dk.
371	433 Brown-med.
357	801 Coffee Brown-dk.
397	762 Pearl Gray-vy. lt.
398	415 Pearl Gray

Step 2: Filet Cross-stitch (1 strand)

900	928 Slate Green-lt.
849	927 Slate Green-med.
876	502 Blue Green

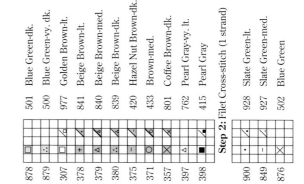

Step 3: Backstitch (1 strand)

849	927 Slate Green-med. (border corners)
379	840 Beige Brown-med. (lettering)
380	839 Beige Brown-dk. (rabbit, horn, jester)
382	3371 Black Brown (baskets)
400	317 Pewter Gray (all else)

Step 4: Smyrna Cross (1 strand)

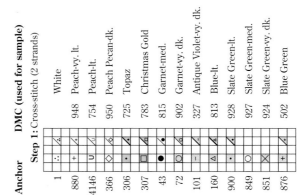

| 43 | 815 Garnet-med. |

Step 5: Beadwork

Mill Hill Beads
▲ 00479 White

Père Noel

SAMPLE
Stitched on white Belfast Linen 32 over 2 threads, the finished design size is 8¼" x 10¾". The fabric was cut 15" x 17".

FABRICS	DESIGN SIZES
Aida 11	11⅞" x 15¾"
Aida 14	9⅜" x 12⅜"
Aida 18	7¼" x 9⅝"
Hardanger 22	6" x 7⅞"

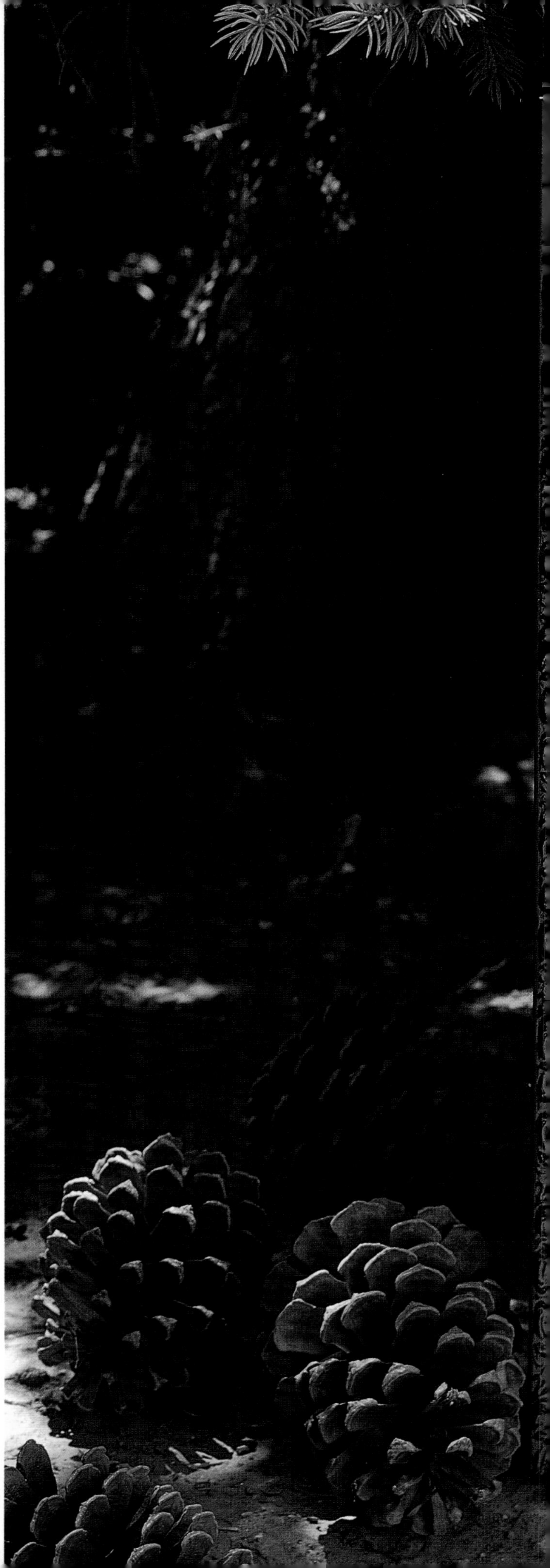

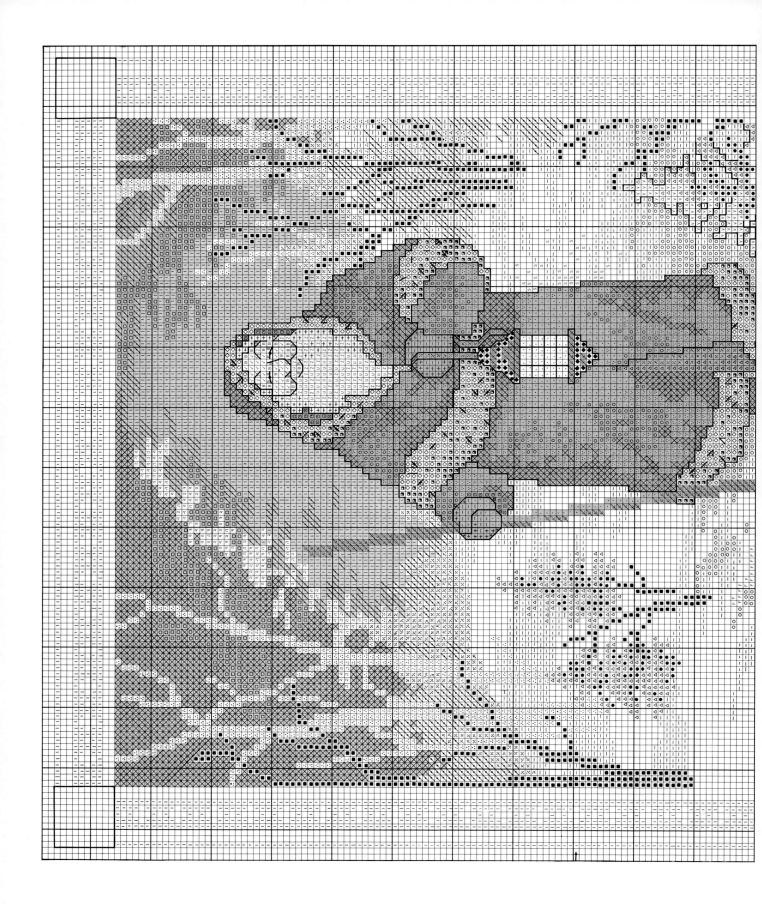

Stitch Count: 131 x 173

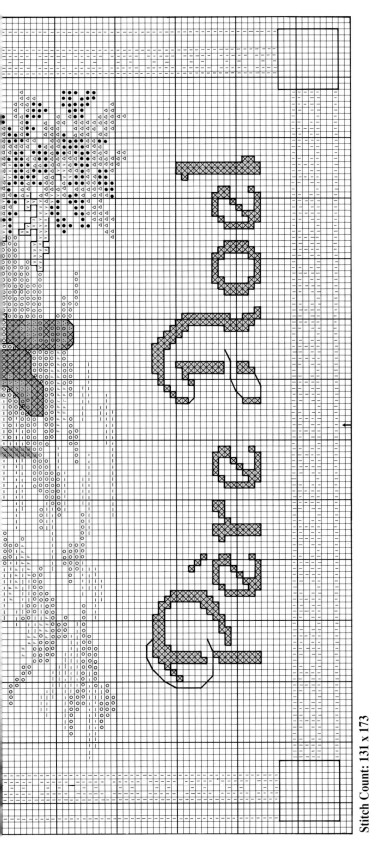

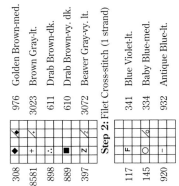

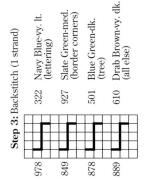

Step 3: Backstitch (1 strand)

	Anchor	DMC	
	978	322	Navy Blue-vy. lt. (lettering)
	849	927	Slate Green-med. (border corners)
	878	501	Blue Green-dk. (tree)
	889	610	Drab Brown-vy. dk. (all else)

	Anchor	DMC	
◆	308	976	Golden Brown-med.
+	8581	3023	Brown Gray-lt.
∴	898	611	Drab Brown-dk.
■	889	610	Drab Brown-vy. dk.
z	397	3072	Beaver Gray-vy. lt.

Step 2: Filet Cross-stitch (1 strand)

	Anchor	DMC	
F	117	341	Blue Violet-lt.
O	145	334	Baby Blue-med.
–	920	932	Antique Blue-lt.

Anchor   DMC (used for sample)

Step 1: Cross-stitch (2 strands)

	Anchor	DMC	
	1		White
∙	386	746	Off White
S	289	307	Lemon
∙	289 324	307 922	Lemon(1 strand) + Copper-lt.(1 strand)
✓	8	353	Peach
B	868	758	Terra Cotta-lt.
–	324	922	Copper-lt.
+	349	921	Copper
O	339	920	Copper-med.
∷	5968	919	Red Copper
X	341	918	Red Copper-dk.
✕	893	224	Shell Pink-lt.
△	894	223	Shell Pink-med.

	Anchor	DMC	
	897	221	Shell Pink-vy. dk.
∙	117	341	Blue Violet-lt.
	145	334	Baby Blue-med.
X	978	322	Navy Blue-vy. lt.
–	920	932	Antique Blue-lt.
	921	931	Antique Blue-med.
	849	927	Slate Green-med.
V	860	3053	Green Gray
⁒	859	522	Fern Green
△	876	502	Blue Green
	878	501	Blue Green-dk.
●	879	500	Blue Green-vy. dk.
◇	942	738	Tan-vy. lt.
	363	436	Tan
	307	977	Golden Brown-lt.

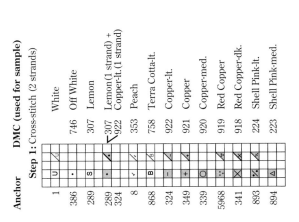

Father Ice

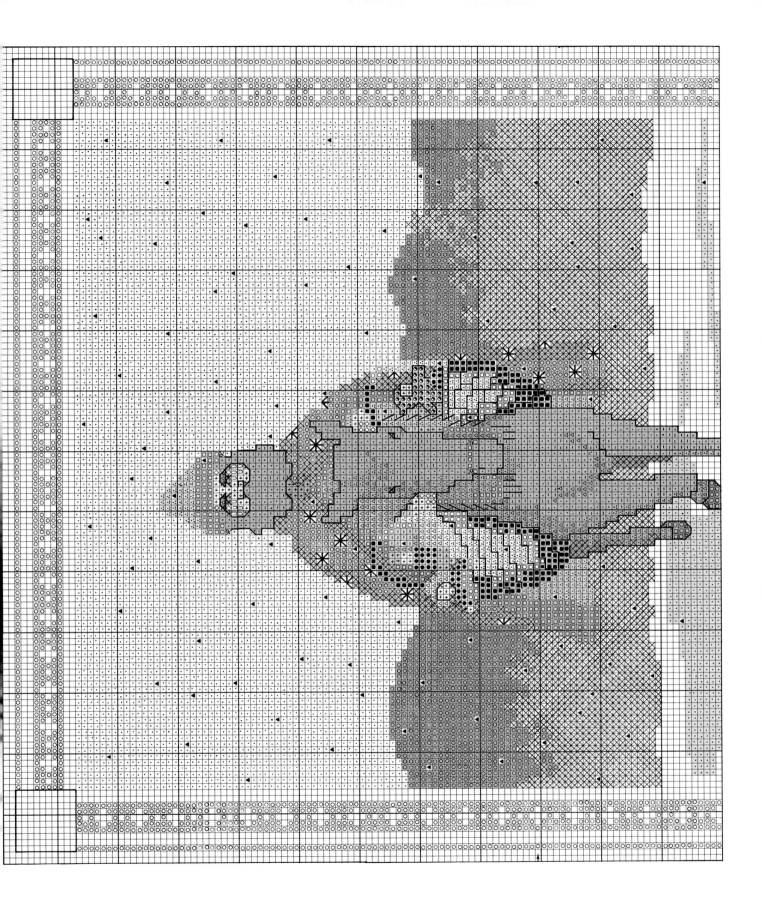

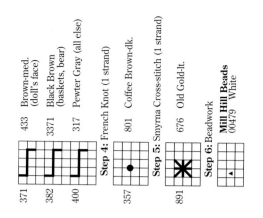

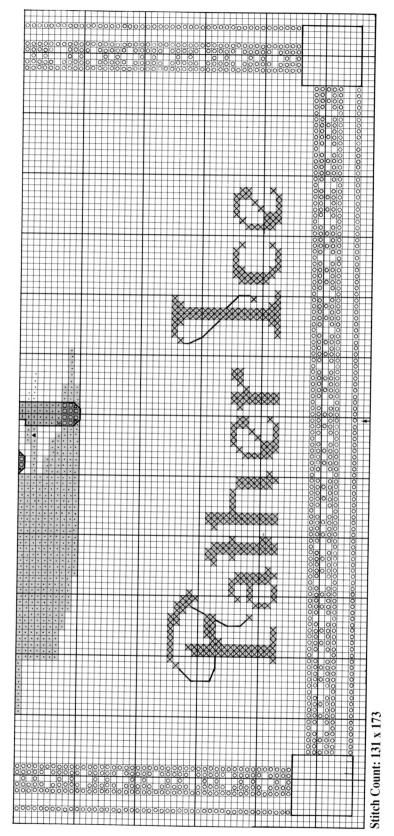

Stitch Count: 131 x 173

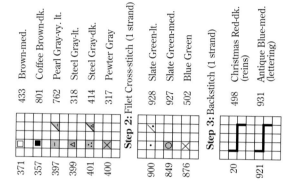

SAMPLE

Stitched on white Belfast Linen 32 over 2 threads, the finished design size is 8¼" x 10¾". The fabric was cut 15" x 17". See Suppliers for Mill Hill beads.

FABRICS	DESIGN SIZES
Aida 11	11⅞" x 15¾"
Aida 14	9⅜" x 12⅜"
Aida 18	7¼" x 9⅝"
Hardanger 22	6" x 7⅞"

Anchor **DMC (used for sample)**

Step 1: Cross-stitch (2 strands)

Anchor	DMC	Color
1		White
778	948	Peach-vy. lt.
880	754	Peach-lt.
4146	950	Peach Pecan-dk.
891	676	Old Gold-lt.
306	725	Topaz
19	817	Coral Red-vy. dk.
20	498	Christmas Red-dk.
43	815	Garnet-med.
130	809	Delft
920	932	Antique Blue-lt.
921	931	Antique Blue-med.
900	928	Slate Green-lt.
849	927	Slate Green-med.
876	502	Blue Green
878	501	Blue Green-dk.
882	407	Pecan
898	611	Drab Brown-dk.
375	420	Hazel Nut Brown-dk.
371	433	Brown-med.
357	801	Coffee Brown-dk.
397	762	Pearl Gray-vy. lt.
399	318	Steel Gray-lt.
401	414	Steel Gray-dk.
400	317	Pewter Gray

Step 2: Filet Cross-stitch (1 strand)

Anchor	DMC	Color
900	928	Slate Green-lt.
849	927	Slate Green-med.
876	502	Blue Green

Step 3: Backstitch (1 strand)

Anchor	DMC	Color
20	498	Christmas Red-dk. (reins)
921	931	Antique Blue-med. (lettering)
371	433	Brown-med. (doll's face)
382	3371	Black Brown (baskets, bear)
400	317	Pewter Gray (all else)

Step 4: French Knot (1 strand)

Anchor	DMC	Color
357	801	Coffee Brown-dk.

Step 5: Smyrna Cross-stitch (1 strand)

Anchor	DMC	Color
891	676	Old Gold-lt.

Step 6: Beadwork

Mill Hill Beads
00479 White

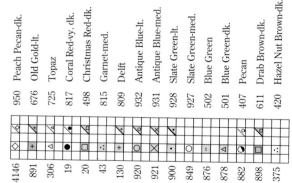

St. Nicholas

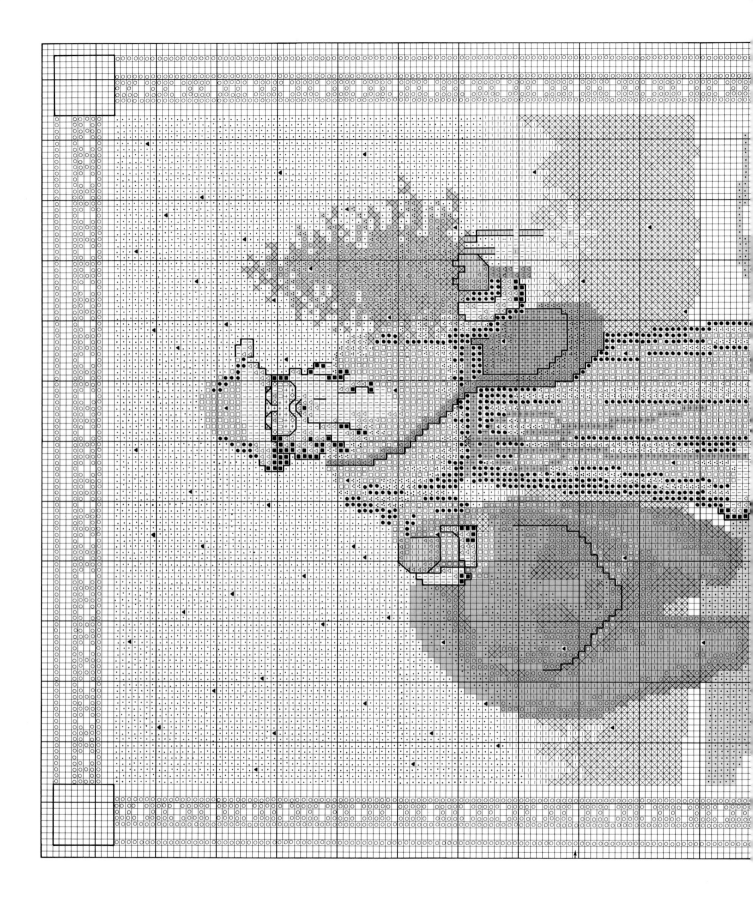

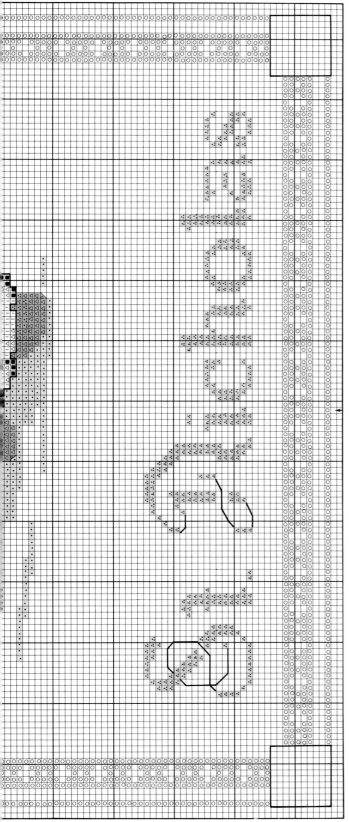

Stitch Count: 131 x 173

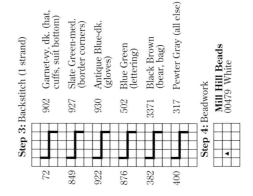

Step 3: Backstitch (1 strand)

	Anchor	DMC	
	72	902	Garnet-vy. dk. (hat, cuffs, suit bottom)
	849	927	Slate Green-med. (border corners)
	922	930	Antique Blue-dk. (gloves)
	876	502	Blue Green (lettering)
	382	3371	Black Brown (bear, bag)
	400	317	Pewter Gray (all else)

Step 4: Beadwork

Mill Hill Beads
00479 White

Anchor	DMC (used for sample)	
		Emerald Green-vy. dk.
229	909	
376	842	Beige Brown-vy. lt.
378	841	Beige Brown-lt.
379	840	Beige Brown-med.
380	839	Beige Brown-dk.
381	838	Beige Brown-vy. dk.
375	420	Hazel Nut Brown-dk.
371	433	Brown-med.
357	801	Coffee Brown-dk.
397	762	Pearl Gray-vy. lt.
398	415	Pearl Gray

Step 2: Filet Cross-stitch (1 strand)

	Anchor	DMC	
	900	928	Slate Green-lt.
	849	927	Slate Green-med.
	876	502	Blue Green

Anchor **DMC (used for sample)**

Step 1: Cross-stitch (2 strands)

Anchor	DMC	
1		White
880	948	Peach-vy. lt.
4146	754	Peach-lt.
366	950	Peach Pecan-dk.
43	815	Garnet-med.
44	814	Garnet-dk.
72	902	Garnet-vy. dk.
900	928	Slate Green-lt.
849	927	Slate Green-med.
920	932	Antique Blue-lt.
921	931	Antique Blue-med.
875	503	Blue Green-med.
876	502	Blue Green
878	501	Blue Green-dk.

SAMPLE

Stitched on white Belfast Linen 32 over 2 threads, the finished design size is 8¼" x 10¾". The fabric was cut 15" x 17". See Suppliers for Mill Hill beads.

FABRICS | DESIGN SIZES

FABRICS	DESIGN SIZES
Aida 11	11⅞" x 15¾"
Aida 14	9⅜" x 12⅜"
Aida 18	7¼" x 9⅝"
Hardanger 22	6" x 7⅞"

Kanaka Loka

SAMPLE
Stitched on white Belfast Linen 32 over 2 threads, the finished design size is 8¼" x 10¾". The fabric was cut 15" x 17".

FABRICS	DESIGN SIZES
Aida 11	11⅞" x 15¾"
Aida 14	9⅜" x 12⅜"
Aida 18	7¼" x 9⅝"
Hardanger 22	6" x 7⅞"

126

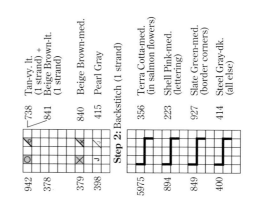

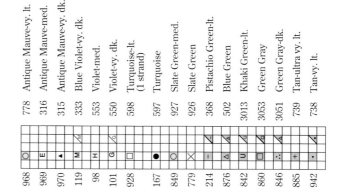

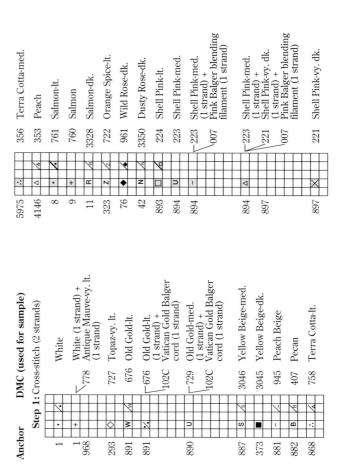

Stitch Count: 131 x 173

Anchor		DMC	
968	⊙	778	Antique Mauve-vy. lt.
969	E	316	Antique Mauve-med.
970	▲	315	Antique Mauve-vy. dk.
119	M	333	Blue Violet-vy. dk.
98	H	553	Violet-med.
101	G	550	Violet-vy. dk.
928	□	598	Turquoise-lt. (1 strand)
167	●	597	Turquoise
849	O	927	Slate Green-med.
779	⊠	926	Slate Green
214		368	Pistachio Green-lt.
876	▲	502	Blue Green
842	U	3013	Khaki Green-lt.
860		3053	Green Gray
846		3051	Green Gray-dk.
885	+	739	Tan-ultra vy. lt.
942		738	Tan-vy. lt.

Anchor		DMC	
942	⊙	738	Tan-vy. lt. (1 strand) +
		841	Beige Brown-lt. (1 strand)
378		840	Beige Brown-med.
379	⊠	415	Pearl Gray
398	J		

Step 2: Backstitch (1 strand)

Anchor		DMC	
356		5975	Terra Cotta-med. (in salmon flowers)
223		894	Shell Pink-med. (lettering)
927		849	Slate Green-med. (border corners)
414		400	Steel Gray-dk. (all else)

Anchor		DMC	
5975	∴	356	Terra Cotta-med.
4146	▲	353	Peach
8	•	761	Salmon-lt.
9	⊿	760	Salmon
11	R	3328	Salmon-dk.
323	Z	722	Orange Spice-lt.
76	◆	961	Wild Rose-dk.
42	N	3350	Dusty Rose-dk.
893	□	224	Shell Pink-lt.
894	U	223	Shell Pink-med.
894	–	223	Shell Pink-med. (1 strand) + 007 Pink Balger blending filament (1 strand)
894	▲	223	Shell Pink-med. (1 strand) +
897		221	Shell Pink-vy. dk. (1 strand) + 007 Pink Balger blending filament (1 strand)
897	⊠	221	Shell Pink-vy. dk.

Anchor — DMC (used for sample)

Step 1: Cross-stitch (2 strands)

Anchor		DMC	
1	•		White
1	+		White (1 strand) +
968		778	Antique Mauve-vy. lt. (1 strand)
293	◇	727	Topaz-vy. lt.
891	W	676	Old Gold-lt.
891	⊠	676	Old Gold-lt. (1 strand) + 102C Vatican Gold Balger cord (1 strand)
890	U	729	Old Gold-med. (1 strand) + 102C Vatican Gold Balger cord (1 strand)
887	S	3046	Yellow Beige-med.
373	■	3045	Yellow Beige-dk.
881	–	945	Peach Beige
882	B	407	Pecan
868	∴	758	Terra Cotta-lt.

Father Frost

129

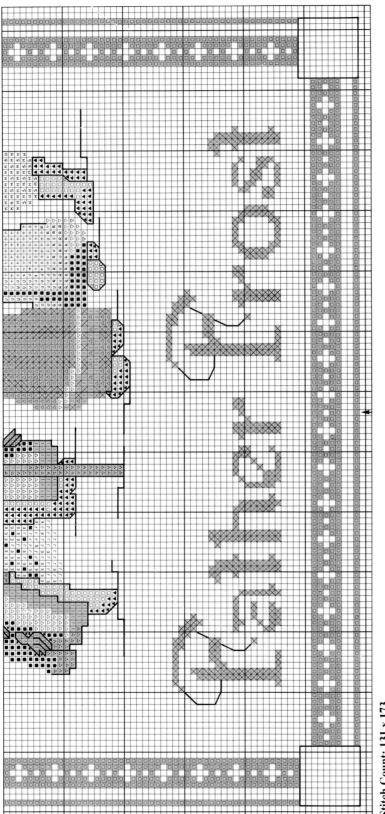

Stitch Count: 131 x 173

SAMPLE

Stitched on white Belfast Linen 32 over 2
threads, the finished design size is 8¼" x 10¾".
The fabric was cut 15" x 17".

FABRICS	**DESIGN SIZES**
Aida 11	11⅞" x 15¾"
Aida 14	9⅜" x 12⅜"
Aida 18	7¼" x 9⅝"
Hardanger 22	6" x 7⅞"

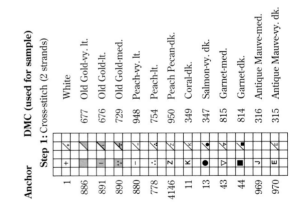

Anchor		DMC (used for sample)
	Step 1:	Cross-stitch (2 strands)
1	+	White
886		677 Old Gold-vy. lt.
891		676 Old Gold-lt.
890		729 Old Gold-med.
880		948 Peach-vy. lt.
778		754 Peach-lt.
4146	Z	950 Peach Pecan-dk.
11	K	349 Coral-dk.
13	●	347 Salmon-vy. dk.
43	▷	815 Garnet-med.
44	■	814 Garnet-dk.
969	J	316 Antique Mauve-med.
970	E	315 Antique Mauve-vy. dk.

870	•	3042 Antique Violet-lt.
871	○	3041 Antique Violet-med.
920	S	932 Antique Blue-lt.
921	R	931 Antique Blue-med.
922	H	930 Antique Blue-dk.
849	□	927 Slate Green-med.
876	△	502 Blue Green
878	✕	501 Blue Green-dk.
879	W	500 Blue Green-vy. dk.
387	✳	822 Beige Gray-lt.
378	□	841 Beige Brown-lt.
379	◄	840 Beige Brown-med.
380	N	839 Beige Brown-dk.
397	U	762 Pearl Gray-vy. lt.

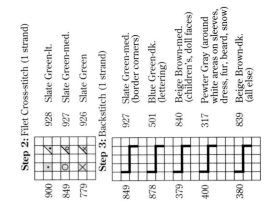

Step 2: Filet Cross-stitch (1 strand)

900	•	928 Slate Green-lt.
849	○	927 Slate Green-med.
779	✕	926 Slate Green

Step 3: Backstitch (1 strand)

849		927 Slate Green-med. (border corners)
878		501 Blue Green-dk. (lettering)
379		840 Beige Brown-med. (children's, doll faces)
400		317 Pewter Gray (around white areas on sleeves, dress, fur, beard, snow)
380		839 Beige Brown-dk. (all else)

Sinter Klaas

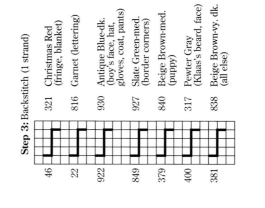

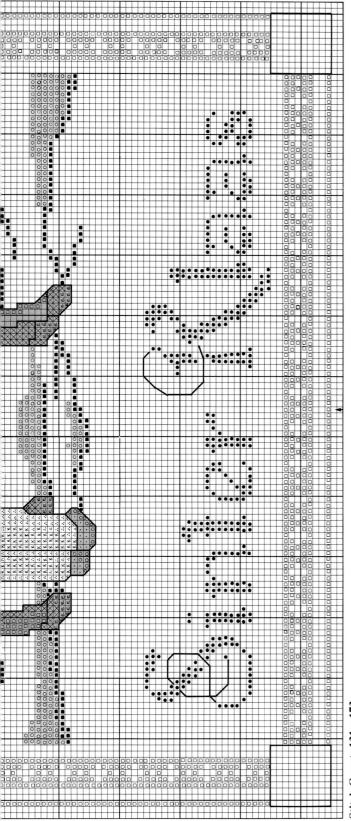

Stitch Count: 131 x 173

SAMPLE

Stitched on white Belfast Linen 32 over 2 threads, the finished design size is 8¼" x 10¾". The fabric was cut 15" x 17".

FABRICS	DESIGN SIZES
Aida 11	11⅞" x 15¾"
Aida 14	9⅜" x 12⅜"
Aida 18	7¼" x 9⅝"
Hardanger 22	6" x 7⅞"

Step 1: Cross-stitch (2 strands)

Anchor	Symbol	DMC (used for sample)	
1	✓		White
1	R		White (1 strand)+
		032	Pearl Balger blending filament (1 strand)
4146	U	754	Peach-lt.
868	Z	758	Terra Cotta-lt.
9	S	760	Salmon
46	△	321	Christmas Red
47	╳	304	Christmas Red-med.
22	●	816	Garnet
44	B	814	Garnet-dk.
128	J	800	Delft-pale
130	N	809	Delft
921	K	931	Antique Blue-med.
922	∴	930	Antique Blue-dk.
849	□	927	Slate Green-med.
210	H	562	Jade-med.
876	I	502	Blue Green
878	▽	501	Blue Green-dk.
879	∵	500	Blue Green-vy. dk.
885	A	739	Tan-ultra vy. lt.
942	M	738	Tan-vy. lt.
307	+	977	Golden Brown-lt.
324	•	922	Copper-lt.
339	○	920	Copper-med.
341	+	918	Red Copper-dk.
903	▲	640	Beige Gray-vy. dk.
378		841	Beige Brown-lt.
379	□	840	Beige Brown-med.
380	╳	839	Beige Brown-dk.
381	E	838	Beige Brown-vy. dk.
397	G	762	Pearl Gray-vy. lt.
398	W	415	Pearl Gray

Step 2: Filet Cross-stitch (1 strand)

Anchor	Symbol	DMC	
159	○	827	Blue-vy. lt.
920	■	932	Antique Blue-lt.
900	•	928	Slate Green-lt.
849	–	927	Slate Green-med.

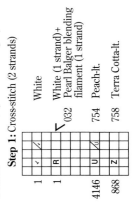

Step 3: Backstitch (1 strand)

Anchor	DMC	
46	321	Christmas Red (fringe, blanket)
22	816	Garnet (lettering)
922	930	Antique Blue-dk. (boy's face, hat, gloves, coat, pants)
849	927	Slate Green-med. (border corners)
379	840	Beige Brown-med. (puppy)
400	317	Pewter Gray (Klaas's beard, face)
381	838	Beige Brown-vy. dk. (all else)

New Creations

Our final chapter introduces brand-new creations from The Vanessa-Ann Collection. You'll find soft florals and geometric shapes that work together to form a delicate look in Floral Elegance. A Home Sweet Home design will fill your home with a springlike feeling of warmth and welcome. Enjoy a taste of The Great Outdoors anytime with our rustic framed piece that depicts nature's wonders, or keep the doctor away with An Apple a Day.

Royal Alphabet

SAMPLE

Stitched on white Belfast Linen 32 over 2 threads, the finished design size is 7½" x 13⅛". The fabric was cut 14" x 20".

FABRICS	DESIGN SIZES
Aida 11	11" x 19⅛"
Aida 14	8⅝" x 15"
Aida 18	6¾" x 11⅝"
Hardanger 22	5½" x 9½"

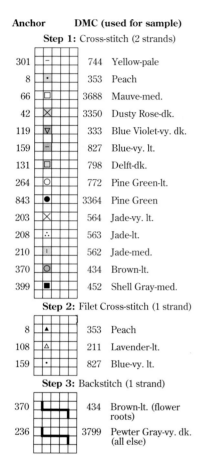

Anchor		DMC (used for sample)	
Step 1: Cross-stitch (2 strands)			
301	–	744	Yellow-pale
8	•	353	Peach
66	□	3688	Mauve-med.
42	⊠	3350	Dusty Rose-dk.
119	▽	333	Blue Violet-vy. dk.
159	▬	827	Blue-vy. lt.
131	□	798	Delft-dk.
264	○	772	Pine Green-lt.
843	●	3364	Pine Green
203	⊠	564	Jade-vy. lt.
208	∴	563	Jade-lt.
210	I	562	Jade-med.
370	◎	434	Brown-lt.
399	■	452	Shell Gray-med.
Step 2: Filet Cross-stitch (1 strand)			
8	▲	353	Peach
108	△	211	Lavender-lt.
159	·	827	Blue-vy. lt.
Step 3: Backstitch (1 strand)			
370		434	Brown-lt. (flower roots)
236		3799	Pewter Gray-vy. dk. (all else)

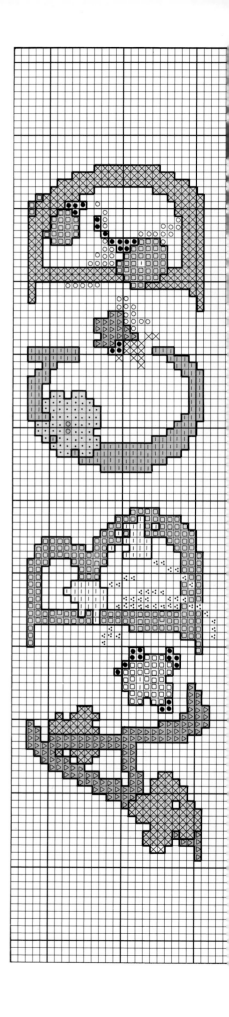

Stitch Count: 121 x 210

An Apple a Day

DELICIOUS

AN AP

A D

KEEPS

DOC

PU

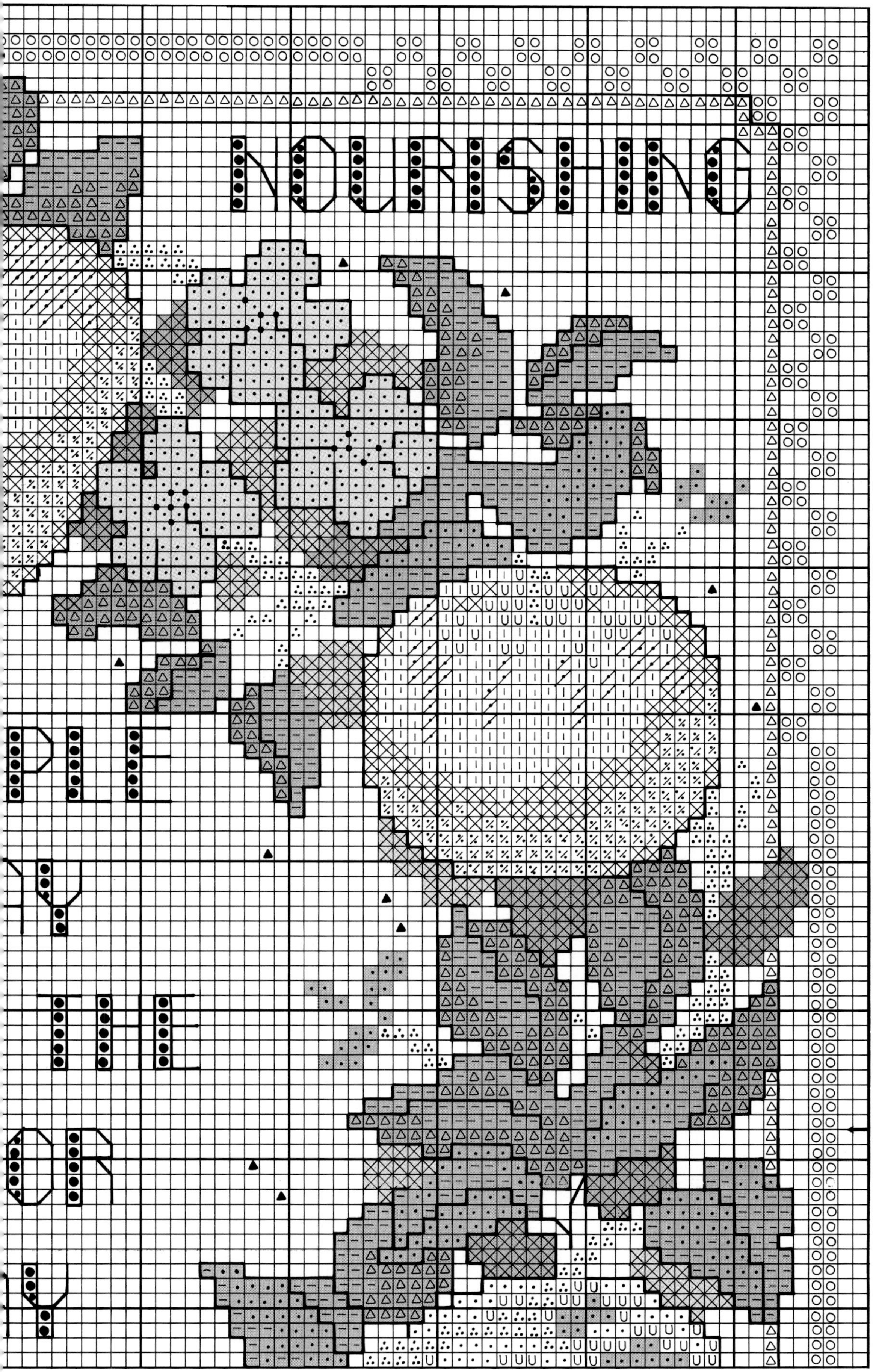
NOURISHING
PLE
Y
THE
OR
Y

Stitch Count: 120 x 148

SAMPLE

Stitched on cream Belfast Linen 32 over 2 threads, the finished design size is 7½" x 9¼". The fabric was cut 14" x 16".

FABRICS	DESIGN SIZES
Aida 11	10⅞" x 13½"
Aida 14	8⅝" x 10⅝"
Aida 18	6⅝" x 8¼"
Hardanger 22	5½" x 6¾"

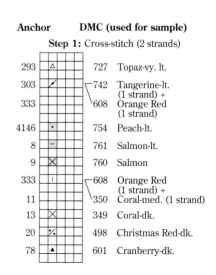

Anchor		DMC (used for sample)	
		Step 1: Cross-stitch (2 strands)	
293	△	727	Topaz-vy. lt.
303	╱	742	Tangerine-lt. (1 strand) +
333		608	Orange Red (1 strand)
4146	·	754	Peach-lt.
8	−	761	Salmon-lt.
9	✕	760	Salmon
333	ı	608	Orange Red (1 strand) +
11		350	Coral-med. (1 strand)
13	✕	349	Coral-dk.
20	⚋	498	Christmas Red-dk.
78	▲	601	Cranberry-dk.

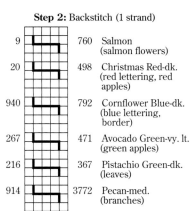

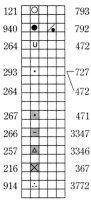
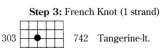

121	O	793	Cornflower Blue-med.
940	● /	792	Cornflower Blue-dk.
264	U	472	Avocado Green-ultra lt.
293	·	727	Topaz-vy. lt. (1 strand) +
264		472	Avocado Green-ultra lt. (1 strand)
267	·	471	Avocado Green-vy. lt.
266	–	3347	Yellow Green-med.
257	△	3346	Hunter Green
216	X	367	Pistachio Green-dk.
914	∴	3772	Pecan-med.

Step 2: Backstitch (1 strand)

9		760	Salmon (salmon flowers)
20		498	Christmas Red-dk. (red lettering, red apples)
940		792	Cornflower Blue-dk. (blue lettering, border)
267		471	Avocado Green-vy. lt. (green apples)
216		367	Pistachio Green-dk. (leaves)
914		3772	Pecan-med. (branches)

Step 3: French Knot (1 strand)

| 303 | ● | 742 | Tangerine-lt. |

Carousel Tiger

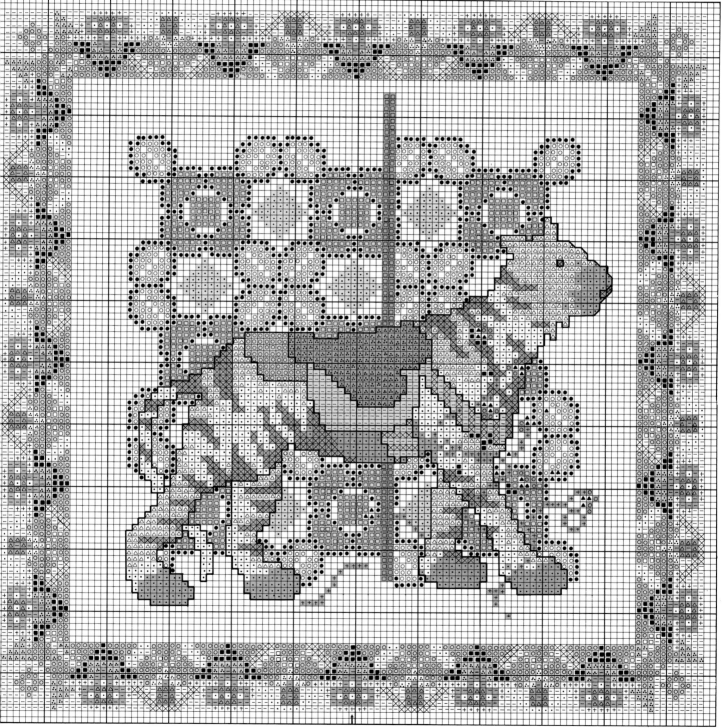

Stitch Count: 113 x 113

SAMPLE

Stitched on white Murano 30 over 2 threads, the finished design size is 7½" x 7½". The fabric was cut 14" x 14".

FABRICS

Aida 11
Aida 14
Aida 18
Hardanger 22

DESIGN SIZES

10¼" x 10¼"
8½" x 8½"
6¼" x 6¼"
5⅛" x 5⅛"

Anchor		DMC (used for sample)	
Step 1: Cross-stitch (2 strands)			
886	·	677	Old Gold-vy. lt.
323	△ ◹	722	Orange Spice-lt.
8	−	761	Salmon-lt.
337	+	3778	Terra Cotta
10	⊘	3712	Salmon-med.
13	▲	347	Salmon-vy. dk.
66	⊠	3688	Mauve-med.
69	∴	3687	Mauve
42	−	3350	Dusty Rose-dk.
95	□	554	Violet-lt.
119	⊘	333	Blue Violet-vy. dk.

42	⊠	3350	Dusty Rose-dk. (1 strand) +
119		333	Blue Violet-vy. dk. (1 strand)
872	⸪	3740	Antique Violet-dk.
928	∴	598	Turquoise-lt.
203	+	564	Jade-vy. lt.
210	■	562	Jade-med.
214	−	368	Pistachio Green-lt.
216	△	367	Pistachio Green-dk.
397	· ◿	762	Pearl Gray-vy. lt.
400	□	414	Steel Gray-dk.
401	⊠ ◹	535	Ash Gray-vy. lt.

Step 2: Filet Cross-stitch (1 strand)

8	·	761	Salmon-lt.
66	○	3688	Mauve-med.
928	□	598	Turquoise-lt.
214	●	368	Pistachio Green-lt.

Step 3: Backstitch (1 strand)

236	⌐	3799	Pewter Gray-vy. dk.

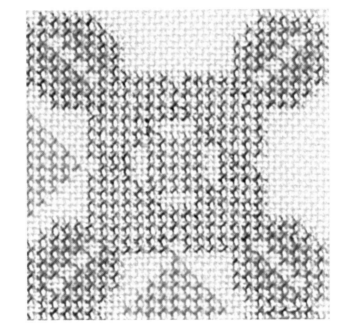

The Great Outdoors

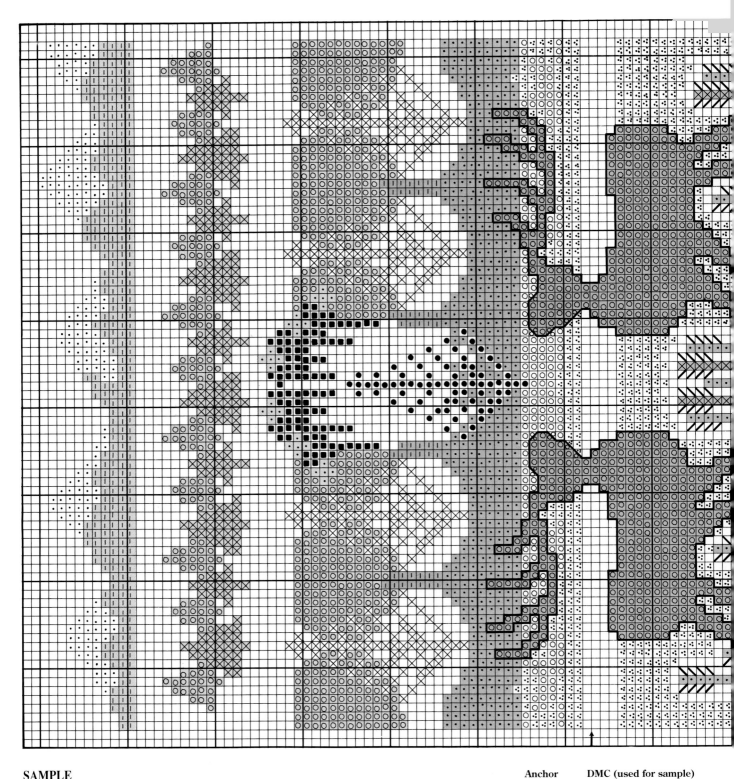

SAMPLE

Stitched on caramel Annabelle 28 over 2 threads, the finished design size is 5⅝" x 9". The fabric was cut 12" x 15".

FABRICS	DESIGN SIZES
Aida 11	7⅛" x 11½"
Aida 14	5⅝" x 9"
Aida 18	4⅜" x 7"
Hardanger 22	3⅝" x 5¾"

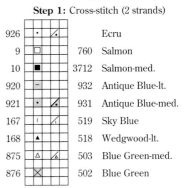

Anchor			DMC (used for sample)	
			Step 1: Cross-stitch (2 strands)	
926				Ecru
9			760	Salmon
10			3712	Salmon-med.
920			932	Antique Blue-lt.
921			931	Antique Blue-med.
167			519	Sky Blue
168			518	Wedgwood-lt.
875			503	Blue Green-med.
876			502	Blue Green

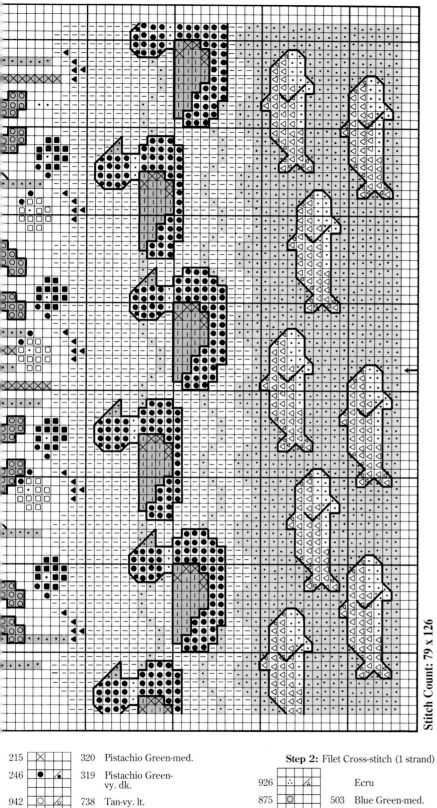

Stitch Count: 79 x 126

215	☒		320	Pistachio Green-med.
246	●	◢	319	Pistachio Green-vy. dk.
942	○	◢	738	Tan-vy. lt.
362	·	◢	437	Tan-lt.
882	–		407	Pecan
914	☒		3772	Pecan-med.
936	○	◢	632	Pecan-dk.

Step 2: Filet Cross-stitch (1 strand)

926	∴	◢		Ecru
875	○		503	Blue Green-med.

Step 3: Backstitch (1 strand)

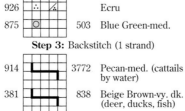

914	⌐		3772	Pecan-med. (cattails by water)
381	⌐		838	Beige Brown-vy. dk. (deer, ducks, fish)

Floral Elegance

Anchor		DMC	(used for sample)
Step 1: Cross-stitch (2 strands)			
300	·	745	Yellow-lt. pale
297	□	743	Yellow-med.
347	▲	402	Mahogany-vy. lt.
24		776	Pink-med.
25	○	3326	Rose-lt.
27	✕	899	Rose-med.
8	ı	761	Salmon-lt.
10	∴	3712	Salmon-med.
13	✕	347	Salmon-vy. dk.
897	●	221	Shell Pink-vy. dk.
869	○	3743	Antique Violet-vy. lt.
975	–	3753	Antique Blue-vy. lt.
264	△	772	Pine Green-lt.
208	✕	563	Jade-lt.
213	□	369	Pistachio Green-vy. lt.
215		320	Pistachio Green-med.
900		928	Slate Green-lt.
Step 2: Backstitch (1 strand)			
347		402	Mahogany-vy. lt. (yellow flowers)
897		221	Shell Pink-vy. dk. (pink and salmon flowers)
215		320	Pistachio Green-med. (leaves)
161		3760	Wedgwood-med. (all else)

Stitch Count: 71 x 98

AMPLE

titched on white Linda 27 over 2 threads, the finished design size is
¼" x 7¼". The fabric was cut 12" x 14".

FABRICS	**DESIGN SIZES**
Aida 11	6½" x 8⅞"
Aida 14	5⅛" x 7"
Aida 18	4" x 5⅛"
Hardanger 22	3¼" x 4½"

Home Sweet Home

SAMPLE
Stitched on white Dublin Linen 25 over 2 threads, the finished design size
is 16½" x 12¾". The fabric was cut 23" x 19".

FABRICS	DESIGN SIZES
Aida 11	18¾" x 14½"
Aida 14	14¾" x 11⅜"
Aida 18	11½" x 8⅞"
Hardanger 22	9⅜" x 7¼"

Stitch Count: 206 x 160

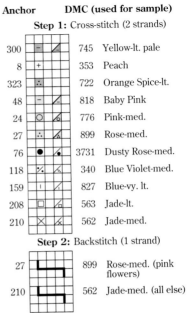

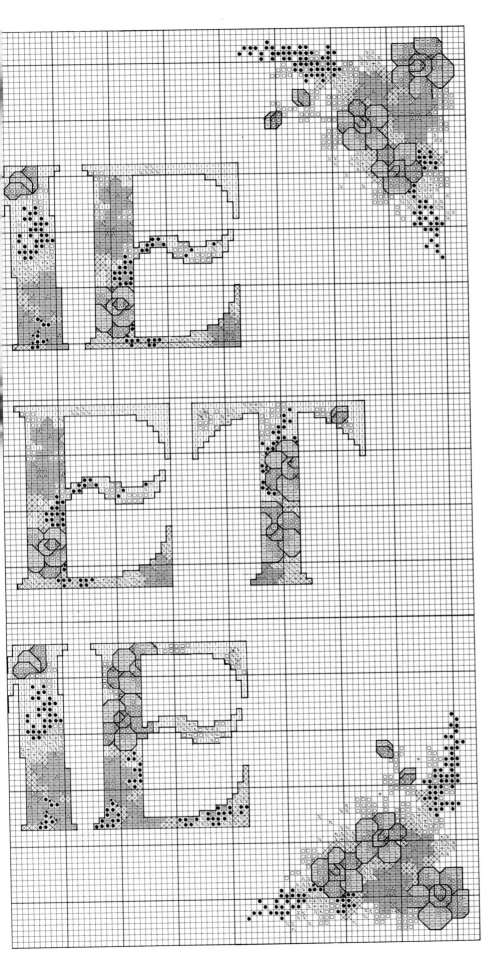

155

...and
they lived
happily
ever after...
DAVID
AND
FRANCES
McMILLAN
AUGUST 25, 1962